Haunted Bridges

Eerie Encounters from The World's Spookiest Structures

By Lee Brickley

Copyright @ Lee Brickley 2023

Contents:

Introduction..5
The Screaming Tunnel Bridge - Niagara Falls, Canada....................7
Goatman's Bridge - Denton, Texas, USA..13
Aokigahara Suicide Forest Bridge - Japan..19
Hell's Bridge - Algoma Township, Michigan, USA..........................25
The Highgate Vampire Bridge – England...31
Overtoun Bridge - Dumbarton, Scotland..37
The Phantom Hitchhiker of Uniondale..43
La Llorona's Crossing - Albuquerque, New Mexico, USA..............49
The Donkey Lady Bridge - San Antonio, Texas, USA.....................55
Clifton Suspension Bridge - Bristol, England...................................61
The Crying Bridge of Malaysia - Penang, Malaysia.........................67
The Ghostly Battle of Stoney Creek - Ontario, Canada..................73
El Muerto of Texas - Refugio, Texas, USA..79
The Vanishing Lady of Barmby Moor – England.............................85
 The Haunted Bridge of Avignon - Avignon, France........................91
The Ghosts of Sydney Harbour Bridge - Sydney, Australia...........97
The Weeping Woman of Malabadi Bridge - Silvan, Turkey........103

The Phantom Car of Tuen Mun Road - Hong Kong..........................109

The Haunted Humber Bridge - Hull, England......................115

The Possessed Doll Bridge - Xochimilco, Mexico............................121

The Enigmatic Eshima Ohashi Bridge - Matsue, Japan.................127

Afterword..133

Introduction

Bridges have long captured the human imagination, symbolising both the physical and metaphorical connections that bring people together. As structures that span vast distances and defy the natural world, they often become the settings for captivating tales of mystery, tragedy, and the supernatural. "Haunted Bridges: Eerie Encounters from The World's Spookiest Structures" takes you on a spine-chilling journey across the globe, revealing the dark secrets and paranormal phenomena that lurk in the shadows of these seemingly ordinary crossings.

In this book, we will delve into the haunted histories of twenty-one bridges, each with its own unique and terrifying tale. From the tormented screams that echo through the Screaming Tunnel Bridge in Niagara Falls to the sinister presence of the Goatman haunting the Old Alton Bridge in Texas, these eerie encounters will send shivers down your spine. Unravel the mysteries of the notorious Aokigahara Suicide Forest Bridge in Japan, where the spirits of the lost linger in the gloomy atmosphere, and discover the harrowing tale of La Llorona's Crossing in Albuquerque, where the tragic spirit of the weeping woman is said to haunt the Juan Tabo Bridge.

As we explore the haunted bridges of the world, we'll unearth fascinating eyewitness accounts and delve into the rich history that surrounds these enigmatic structures. The stories we'll uncover range from ancient folklore and tragic events to supernatural encounters that defy explanation. Whether you're a believer in the paranormal or a sceptic seeking thrilling tales, "Haunted Bridges" promises to intrigue, entertain, and perhaps even keep you up at night.

So, prepare to embark on a spine-tingling journey, as we traverse the world's spookiest structures and uncover the chilling secrets that lie within. Will you dare to cross these haunted bridges?

The Screaming Tunnel Bridge - Niagara Falls, Canada

Niagara Falls, one of the world's most captivating natural wonders, straddles the border between the United States and Canada. This breathtaking destination, known for the thunderous roar of the falls themselves, holds a lesser-known secret just a short distance away from the hustle and bustle of the tourist crowds. In the shadows of the surrounding area, the Screaming Bridge has captured the attention of locals and visitors alike with its eerie legend of a tormented spirit whose screams still resonate through the night.

The Screaming Bridge, an old iron structure spanning the width of a small creek, is located in a secluded area of Niagara Falls, Ontario. Built in the early 20th century, the bridge served as a passageway for local farmers and their livestock as they travelled across the creek. As the years passed, the rural landscape transformed with the growth of industry and development, and the bridge was eventually abandoned. The passage of time has left the bridge weathered and worn, adding to its eerie and mysterious atmosphere.

It is here, amid the rusting iron and decaying wood, that a chilling legend has taken root. According to local lore, a young girl met a horrific fate on or near the bridge, and her anguished screams have echoed through the area ever since. While there are several variations of the story, each centres around the tragic and untimely death of a young girl whose restless spirit is said to haunt the bridge.

One version of the tale recounts the story of a girl who lived in a nearby farmhouse in the early 20th century. A devastating fire engulfed her home, and she managed to flee the inferno, her clothes and body ravaged by the flames. Disoriented and terrified, she stumbled through the darkness, seeking safety and solace on the bridge. It was there that she succumbed to her injuries, her agonised screams echoing through the night.

Another iteration of the story tells of a brutal murder. In this chilling account, the young girl was viciously attacked by an unknown assailant near the bridge. Her terrified screams pierced the night as she fought for her life, but ultimately, she was overpowered and left to die on the cold, hard ground. The echoes of her final moments are said to haunt the area to this day, serving as a stark reminder of her tragic end.

Despite the variations in the story, one element remains consistent: the tormented spirit of a young girl whose chilling screams can still be heard near the Screaming Bridge. Over the years, this eerie tale has attracted curious thrill-seekers and paranormal enthusiasts who venture to the bridge in search of the supernatural. Many have reported unexplained occurrences, from disembodied screams and ghostly apparitions to sudden drops in temperature and feelings of being watched.

One eyewitness account comes from a local resident named Sarah, who visited the bridge with a group of friends late one night. As they stood on the bridge, they heard what sounded like a distant, anguished scream. They all froze in terror, straining their ears to determine the source of the sound. Just as suddenly as it had started, the scream stopped, leaving them all shaken and eager to leave the area.

Another visitor, James, claimed to have seen a ghostly figure on the bridge as he approached it one evening. The pale, transparent figure of a young girl appeared to be standing at the edge of the bridge, staring out into the darkness. As he got closer, the apparition vanished, leaving him with an overwhelming sense of sadness and despair.

Regardless of whether one believes in the paranormal or not, the legend of the Screaming Bridge of Niagara Falls continues to captivate the imagination and draw in those seeking a thrilling encounter with the unknown. The tragic tale of the young girl and her tormented spirit serves as a chilling reminder of the darker side of human history, and the bridge itself stands as a haunting monument to her suffering.

Over the years, the Screaming Bridge has become a source of local folklore and an intriguing destination for paranormal enthusiasts and sceptics alike. Whether visitors come to pay their respects to the lost soul or to challenge their own fears, the bridge and its chilling legend remain a lasting testament to the unexplained mysteries that permeate our world.

As we continue to explore the haunted bridges of the world, we will encounter even more harrowing tales of tragedy, loss, and the supernatural. Each bridge has its own unique story, a tapestry woven from the threads of history, folklore, and the unexplained. The Screaming Bridge of Niagara Falls is just one of many eerie encounters that await us on our journey, but the chilling screams of a tormented spirit will undoubtedly linger in our minds as we venture further into the shadows of the world's spookiest structures.

Goatman's Bridge - Denton, Texas, USA

In the heart of Denton County, Texas, a seemingly ordinary bridge stands as a testament to one of the area's most chilling legends. The Old Alton Bridge, also known as Goatman's Bridge, spans the Hickory Creek and was once an essential transportation link for the local community. Today, the bridge is closed to vehicle traffic, but its haunted history and the sinister presence of the Goatman continue to draw curious visitors seeking an encounter with the supernatural.

Constructed in 1884, the Old Alton Bridge was a vital connection between the towns of Denton and Alton. It served as a primary thoroughfare for farmers and merchants, who relied on the iron truss bridge to transport their goods across the creek. As time went on, the town of Alton diminished, and the city of Denton absorbed the surrounding area. The bridge eventually fell out of use and was closed to vehicular traffic in 2001. Despite the passage of time and the march of progress, the bridge has remained, a ghostly relic of a bygone era.

It is here, amid the creaking iron and timeworn wood, that the sinister legend of the Goatman took root. The Goatman, a half-man, half-goat creature, is said to have haunted the Old Alton Bridge and its surrounding area for generations. There are several versions of the Goatman's origin story, each more chilling than the last. One of the most popular tales involves a local African-American goat farmer named Oscar Washburn.

Washburn, known as a kind and honest man, lived with his family near the bridge in the early 20th century. He made a living by raising and selling goats, earning him the nickname "The Goatman." As his reputation grew, so did the resentment and anger of some local residents, who were deeply entrenched in the racism and prejudice of the time. One fateful night in 1938, a mob of Klansmen, seeking to put an end to Washburn's success, abducted him from his home and dragged him to the bridge.

The mob hung Washburn from the side of the bridge by a noose, fully intending to watch him die. But when they looked over the railing to confirm their brutal act, they found the noose empty, and Washburn had vanished. Panic-stricken, the mob returned to Washburn's home and murdered his wife and children in a final act of vengeance. Washburn's body was never found, but legend has it that he was transformed into the vengeful Goatman, a monstrous hybrid creature bent on terrorising those who dare to cross his bridge.

Visitors to the Old Alton Bridge have reported numerous paranormal experiences over the years, including sightings of the Goatman himself. The creature is often described as having the body of a man and the head of a goat, complete with twisted horns and glowing red eyes. Many have reported an overwhelming sense of dread and unease when approaching the bridge, as well as sudden drops in temperature and unexplained sounds.

Eyewitness accounts of the Goatman's Bridge are as numerous as they are chilling. One visitor, a man named Mark, recounted his experience walking across the bridge late one night. As he reached the middle of the bridge, he heard a guttural growl and felt an icy chill envelop him. Terrified, he looked around and saw a pair of glowing red eyes staring back at him from the darkness. Convinced that he had encountered the Goatman, Mark fled the bridge and never returned.

Another account comes from a group of teenagers who decided to visit the bridge on a dare. As they approached the bridge, they began to hear strange noises in the distance, almost like the bleating of a goat. Unnerved but determined to prove their bravery, the group continued across the bridge. Suddenly, a dark figure appeared at the far end, its red eyes glaring menacingly. The teens, overwhelmed with terror, turned and ran, only to hear the sound of hooves thundering behind them. They escaped the bridge unharmed but were left with a haunting memory that would stay with them for the rest of their lives.

The Goatman's Bridge has also become a popular destination for paranormal investigators seeking to document and understand the strange phenomena that occur there. Many investigators have recorded inexplicable fluctuations in electromagnetic fields, as well as unexplained cold spots and disembodied voices. Some have even captured mysterious figures in photographs and video, sparking further debate and fascination with the legend of the Goatman.

As we delve deeper into the haunted history of the Old Alton Bridge, we must also consider the psychological and social factors that contribute to its enduring legend. The tragic tale of Oscar Washburn and his family serves as a stark reminder of the dark undercurrents of racism and hatred that plagued American society in the early 20th century. The transformation of Washburn into the vengeful Goatman can be seen as a symbol of the collective guilt and fear that arose from these injustices. Whether or not the Goatman is a genuine supernatural entity, the bridge and its legend serve as an unsettling mirror reflecting the darker aspects of human nature.

The haunted history of the Goatman's Bridge, like the Screaming Tunnel Bridge in Niagara Falls, reveals the complex and often unnerving relationship between the paranormal and the human psyche. As we continue our journey through the world's spookiest structures, we will encounter even more fascinating tales of tragedy, mystery, and the unexplained. From the haunted bridges of Japan to the ghostly crossings of Albuquerque, each bridge has a story to tell, a chilling secret waiting to be uncovered.

In the chapters to come, we will traverse the globe, investigating the haunted bridges that have captivated the imagination of countless generations. As we examine the rich history and eerie phenomena that surround these enigmatic structures, we will come face-to-face with the supernatural forces that defy explanation.

Aokigahara Suicide Forest Bridge - Yamanashi Prefecture, Japan

In the shadow of Mount Fuji lies a dense, sprawling forest known as Aokigahara, a place shrouded in mystery and dark legends. This foreboding forest has earned the moniker "Suicide Forest," as it is notorious for being one of the world's most popular locations for people to take their own lives. On the outskirts of this tragic woodland, there is a bridge that carries its own haunting tale, the Aokigahara Suicide Forest Bridge. This seemingly unremarkable crossing has become entwined with the dark history of its surroundings, with numerous paranormal encounters and eerie phenomena reported by those who have dared to cross its threshold.

The Aokigahara Suicide Forest Bridge, located in Yamanashi

Prefecture, was built in the early 1900s as a means of connecting the nearby villages and providing access to the forest for both locals and visitors. The bridge's construction coincided with a period of rapid industrialization in Japan, which saw the expansion of roads, railways, and other infrastructure. It was during this time that the dark reputation of the Aokigahara Forest began to take root, with tales of ghostly apparitions and strange occurrences becoming more and more frequent.

While the Aokigahara Forest has long been associated with death and the paranormal, the origins of this association can be traced back even further in Japanese history. The forest is said to be haunted by the spirits of "yūrei," the ghosts of those who have died with deep sadness or unresolved issues in their lives. These spirits are believed to wander the forest, seeking solace and resolution, but are unable to find peace, trapped in a limbo between the world of the living and the afterlife. The Aokigahara Forest's reputation as a suicide hotspot has only served to heighten the fear and superstition surrounding the area, with many believing that the souls of those who have taken their own lives now add to the ranks of the restless yūrei.

The Aokigahara Suicide Forest Bridge has become inextricably linked with the tragic history of the forest itself, with many claiming to have encountered the spirits of the lost as they cross its timeworn planks. One such encounter involves a young woman named Yuki, who visited the bridge with a group of friends as part of a dare. As they approached the bridge, they could feel the temperature drop and an oppressive sense of unease settle over them. Yuki, determined to prove her bravery, stepped onto the bridge first, only to be confronted by the apparition of a woman dressed in white. The ghostly figure's face bore an expression of deep anguish, and as she reached out towards Yuki, her friends could hear her sobs echoing through the air. Terrified, the group fled, leaving the spirit behind on the bridge.

Another chilling account comes from a local man named Hiroshi, who decided to visit the bridge one evening after hearing the stories of hauntings and paranormal phenomena. As he walked across the bridge, he noticed a strange, flickering light off in the distance, deep within the forest. Intrigued, he decided to investigate, only to find himself drawn deeper and deeper into the tangled woods. The further he went, the more disoriented he became, and he soon realised that he was lost. As panic set in, Hiroshi began to hear whispers all around him, voices that seemed to be urging him to take his own life. Desperate, he called out for help, and it was only then that the voices ceased and he was able to find his way back to the bridge. Shaken by his experience, Hiroshi became convinced that the spirits of the forest had been attempting to lure him to his death, using the bridge as a gateway to their haunted realm.

Visitors to the Aokigahara Suicide Forest Bridge have also reported a range of other paranormal phenomena, including sudden drops in temperature, unexplained sounds, and feelings of being watched or followed. Some have even claimed to have seen shadowy figures lurking in the trees on either side of the bridge, their eyes seeming to glow with an unnatural light. These unsettling encounters have led many to believe that the bridge itself is a conduit for the restless spirits of the Aokigahara Forest, a place where the boundary between the living and the dead is at its thinnest.

The history of the Aokigahara Suicide Forest Bridge is a tragic one, with countless lives lost in the depths of the surrounding woods. It is perhaps this legacy of pain and despair that has imbued the bridge with its eerie atmosphere, attracting the souls of the lost and the tormented. As the number of suicides in the forest continues to rise, so too does the bridge's sinister reputation, with each new victim adding to the weight of sorrow that hangs over the area.

There are those who have sought to understand the forces at work on the Aokigahara Suicide Forest Bridge, with paranormal investigators, psychics, and even government officials attempting to unravel the mysteries of the haunted crossing. Some have pointed to the presence of high levels of magnetic activity in the area, which is said to interfere with compasses and other navigational devices. This has led to speculation that the bridge may be situated on a "ley line," a sort of spiritual energy grid that connects sites of significance around the world. It is thought that these ley lines may act as channels for supernatural forces, providing a conduit for the restless spirits of the forest to make their presence felt on the bridge.

Others believe that the haunting of the Aokigahara Suicide Forest Bridge is the result of the immense psychic energy generated by the countless tragedies that have taken place in the area. According to this theory, the bridge has become a sort of "psychic battery," storing the emotional turmoil and anguish of the many lost souls who have ended their lives in the forest. This accumulated energy is said to manifest itself in the form of paranormal phenomena, with the bridge serving as a focal point for the restless spirits that are drawn to its dark history.

Regardless of the cause, the Aokigahara Suicide Forest Bridge remains a chilling reminder of the deep despair and sorrow that permeates the very air of the surrounding woodland. Its haunted reputation has become a part of local folklore, with many residents of the nearby villages avoiding the bridge altogether, fearing the sinister forces that are said to reside there. For those who dare to cross the Aokigahara Suicide Forest Bridge, the experience is one that is not easily forgotten, as they come face to face with the lingering spirits of the lost and the tormented.

In the eerie, unsettling world of haunted bridges, the Aokigahara Suicide Forest Bridge stands as a testament to the power of human emotion and the darkness that lies hidden beneath the surface of even the most seemingly ordinary structures. As we continue our journey through the world's spookiest structures, we must remember that each bridge carries not only the weight of its physical construction, but also the weight of the countless stories and experiences that have unfolded upon its planks. The Aokigahara Suicide Forest Bridge serves as a stark reminder of the pain and suffering that can permeate even the most innocuous of places, and the eerie encounters that await those who dare to venture too close.

Hell's Bridge - Algoma Township, Michigan, USA

In the quiet rural community of Algoma Township, Michigan, there lies a seemingly ordinary bridge with a dark and sinister history. Known as Hell's Bridge, this unassuming structure spans the Rogue River, providing passage for those who dare to cross it. But beneath the surface of this quaint crossing lies a gruesome tale of murder, deceit, and supernatural terror, the echoes of which still haunt the area to this day.

The legend of Hell's Bridge begins in the mid-19th century with a man named Elias Friske. Friske was a resident of Algoma Township and was well-regarded by his neighbours for his devout religious beliefs and charitable nature. However, unbeknownst to the people of Algoma, Friske harboured a dark and twisted secret. He believed that the souls of the children in his community were tainted with sin, and that it was his divine duty to cleanse them of their wickedness. His twisted mission led him to commit a series of heinous crimes that would forever stain the town's history and earn him a place among the most feared figures in local folklore.

Friske's descent into madness began with the kidnapping of several children from the township. He lured the unsuspecting youngsters deep into the woods, where he bound their hands and feet with rope and led them to the banks of the Rogue River. It was there that he committed his unspeakable acts, slaying the children one by one and casting their lifeless bodies into the churning waters below. His brutal spree continued for several months, with each new victim adding to the ever-growing list of the damned.

The townspeople of Algoma eventually discovered the terrible truth about Friske and his horrific crimes. A search party was assembled, and they tracked him down to the banks of the Rogue River, where they found him standing on a wooden bridge, his clothes stained with the blood of his victims. Friske was captured and brought to justice, but his dark legacy would not end with his death. The bridge where he had carried out his gruesome deeds soon gained a reputation for being haunted, with locals claiming to hear the tormented cries of the murdered children echoing through the trees at night. And so, Hell's Bridge was born.

Over the years, countless visitors have flocked to Hell's Bridge to experience the paranormal phenomena that are said to plague the area. Many have reported feeling a sudden drop in temperature as they approach the bridge, as well as an overwhelming sense of dread that seems to envelop the surrounding woods. Others have claimed to see shadowy figures lurking among the trees, their eyes glowing with an unearthly light. But perhaps the most chilling encounters are those involving the ghostly voices of the murdered children themselves, their cries for help and mercy echoing through the night.

One such encounter was reported by a local man named James, who visited Hell's Bridge with a group of friends in the early 2000s. As they crossed the bridge, they heard what sounded like the faint sobbing of a child coming from the woods nearby. The group decided to investigate and followed the sound deeper into the trees, where they stumbled upon a small clearing. It was there that they encountered the apparition of a young girl, her face twisted in anguish as she sobbed uncontrollably. The group watched in horror as the spirit vanished before their eyes, leaving them shaken and convinced that they had witnessed the restless soul of one of Friske's victims.

Another eerie account comes from a woman named Sarah, who visited Hell's Bridge with her husband in 2015. As they stood on the bridge, they both experienced a sudden chill and the sensation of an unseen presence watching them. Deciding to leave, they quickly made their way back to their car, only to hear footsteps following closely behind them. When they turned to look, there was nothing there, but the footsteps continued, growing louder and more menacing as they hurried to their vehicle. Sarah and her husband managed to escape the area unharmed, but the chilling encounter left them with no doubt that Hell's Bridge was indeed haunted.

Hell's Bridge has also attracted the attention of paranormal investigators, who have ventured to the site in search of evidence of the supernatural. One such investigation was conducted by a team from the Michigan Paranormal Research Association (MPRA). The MPRA spent several nights at Hell's Bridge, using a variety of equipment to document any paranormal activity that might occur. Over the course of their investigation, they captured several audio recordings that seemed to contain the faint sounds of children crying, as well as unexplained whispers and even the name "Elias" spoken by an unknown voice. The team also experienced several instances of their equipment malfunctioning in inexplicable ways, further fueling speculation that the bridge is haunted by the spirits of Friske's victims.

The history of Hell's Bridge is undeniably tragic and disturbing, with the brutal actions of Elias Friske casting a long shadow over the community of Algoma Township. However, it is also a testament to the power of folklore and the human imagination, as the tales of supernatural terror that have sprung up around the bridge continue to captivate and terrify those who hear them. Whether one believes in the paranormal or simply enjoys a spine-chilling story, the legend of Hell's Bridge offers a chilling glimpse into the darkness that can reside within the human heart.

The Highgate Vampire Bridge - Highgate Cemetery, England

In the heart of London, England, lies a bridge shrouded in mystery, supernatural intrigue, and spine-chilling terror. The Swains Lane Bridge, located near the iconic Highgate Cemetery, has long been the subject of eerie encounters and terrifying tales of the unexplained. At the centre of these stories is the infamous Highgate Vampire, a sinister figure that has haunted the imaginations of Londoners for generations. In this chapter, we will delve into the haunted history of the Highgate Vampire Bridge, exploring the chilling encounters that have made it one of the most feared structures in the world.

Highgate Cemetery, established in 1839, is one of London's most famous burial grounds and a true architectural marvel. Its Gothic-style tombs, mausoleums, and monuments have made it the final resting place for some of the city's most notable figures.

However, it is also a place of darkness and mystery, with countless stories of supernatural sightings and unexplained occurrences that have long captured the public's fascination. Among these tales, the legend of the Highgate Vampire stands out as one of the most chilling and captivating.

The story of the Highgate Vampire is believed to have begun in the late 1960s, when reports of strange sightings and bizarre happenings near the Swains Lane Bridge began to emerge. Local residents claimed to have seen a tall, dark figure with piercing red eyes lurking in the shadows of the bridge, seemingly watching those who dared to pass beneath it. Others reported feeling an intense sense of dread and unease when approaching the area, as if some malevolent force was lurking nearby.

As word of these eerie encounters spread, paranormal enthusiasts and vampire hunters alike were drawn to the bridge, hoping to catch a glimpse of the mysterious figure and perhaps even vanquish the evil presence that seemed to haunt it. The most famous of these investigations was led by British occultist David Farrant, who claimed to have seen the Highgate Vampire himself during a visit to the cemetery in 1970.

Farrant's chilling account of his encounter with the creature sparked a media frenzy, with newspapers across the country running stories on the Highgate Vampire and the supernatural events that seemed to plague the Swains Lane Bridge. As more and more people flocked to the area in search of the vampire, additional eyewitness accounts began to emerge, further fueling the legend.

One such account comes from a man named John, who claimed to have seen the Highgate Vampire while walking near the bridge in the early hours of the morning. John described the creature as a tall, gaunt figure dressed in black, with pale skin and blood-red eyes that seemed to glow with an unearthly light. As he watched, the figure seemed to glide effortlessly over the ground, disappearing into the shadows beneath the bridge.

Another harrowing encounter was reported by a woman named Elizabeth, who was visiting the cemetery in the late 1970s. As she approached the Swains Lane Bridge, she claimed to have been overcome by an intense feeling of terror, as if some malevolent presence was nearby. Suddenly, she saw a dark figure standing on the bridge, its eyes fixed on her with an unsettling intensity. Before she could react, the figure vanished, leaving her shaken and convinced that she had come face-to-face with the infamous Highgate Vampire.

These stories and countless others have made the Highgate Vampire Bridge one of the most notorious haunted structures in the world. Some believe that the vampire is the spirit of a mediaeval nobleman who practised the dark arts and was buried in the cemetery, while others contend that it is the restless soul of a Romanian nobleman who was interred in the cemetery in the 19th century. Regardless of its origins, the legend of the Highgate Vampire has become a fixture of local folklore, inspiring fear and fascination in equal measure.

In recent years, paranormal investigators have continued to be drawn to the Swains Lane Bridge, seeking to uncover the truth behind the chilling stories of the Highgate Vampire. These intrepid explorers have employed a variety of techniques and equipment, from infrared cameras to electronic voice recorders, in their quest to document the supernatural phenomena that are said to occur in the area.

One notable investigation was conducted by a team of paranormal researchers from the London Ghost Hunters Society (LGHS). Over the course of several nights, the LGHS team set up a series of experiments in and around the Swains Lane Bridge, hoping to capture evidence of the Highgate Vampire or any other paranormal activity. During their investigation, the team reported numerous instances of unexplained temperature fluctuations and electromagnetic field disturbances, as well as several sightings of mysterious orbs and shadowy figures.

Perhaps the most compelling piece of evidence captured by the LGHS team was an audio recording that appeared to contain the sound of a disembodied voice whispering the word "vampire." While this recording is far from definitive proof of the Highgate Vampire's existence, it adds to the growing body of evidence that suggests there may be more to the legend than mere folklore and urban myth.

The Highgate Vampire Bridge is a chilling testament to the power of supernatural stories and the enduring fascination that they hold for people all around the world. The tales of the vampire and the eerie encounters that have occurred at the Swains Lane Bridge have become part of the fabric of London's haunted history, capturing the imaginations of both believers and sceptics alike.

Overtoun Bridge - Dumbarton, Scotland

Tucked away in the lush, rolling countryside of Dumbarton, Scotland, lies a picturesque and seemingly unassuming structure known as the Overtoun Bridge. A majestic, Victorian-era granite bridge that stretches over a serene, meandering river, the Overtoun Bridge is an architectural gem that embodies the charm and grace of its surroundings. Yet, beneath its elegant facade lies a dark and chilling secret – a series of mysterious canine deaths that have plagued the bridge for decades, as well as numerous reports of an enigmatic presence that seems to haunt its very stones.

Constructed in 1895 by renowned architect H.E. Milner, the Overtoun Bridge was designed to provide access to the nearby Overtoun House, a stately Victorian manor that has since been converted into a Christian centre. The bridge itself is an impressive feat of engineering, with its imposing granite arches and ornate balustrades a testament to the skill and craftsmanship of the builders who created it.

Despite its striking beauty and historic significance, the Overtoun Bridge has gained a more sinister reputation in recent years, due to the inexplicable and tragic phenomenon of dogs leaping to their deaths from its parapets. Since the 1950s, it is estimated that over 50 dogs have met their end at the bridge, with some reports suggesting that the number may be as high as 600. The dogs, seemingly compelled by an unseen force, leap from the bridge without warning, plunging 50 feet to the rocky riverbed below. Incredibly, this phenomenon appears to occur almost exclusively on the right-hand side of the bridge, further deepening the mystery surrounding these tragic events.

The unexplained nature of these canine deaths has led to a wealth of speculation and conjecture, with theories ranging from the scientific to the supernatural. Some believe that the dogs are drawn to the bridge by the scent of mink or other animals in the area, while others suggest that the unique acoustic properties of the bridge may be disorienting the dogs, causing them to leap in confusion. However, neither of these theories fully explains the strange specificity of the phenomenon – namely, the fact that the dogs only seem to jump from the right-hand side of the bridge.

Inevitably, the mysterious deaths at the Overtoun Bridge have given rise to a number of paranormal theories, with many believing that the bridge is haunted by an enigmatic presence that lures the dogs to their doom. This belief has been fueled by numerous eyewitness accounts of strange and unexplained happenings at the bridge, as well as a pervasive sense of unease that seems to linger in the air.

One such account comes from a woman named Mary, who was walking her dog near the bridge in the early 2000s. As they approached the bridge, Mary noticed that her usually placid dog suddenly became agitated and seemed to be drawn to the right-hand side of the structure. Despite her best efforts to restrain him, the dog broke free from her grasp and leaped over the parapet, narrowly avoiding a tragic fate as Mary managed to grab his collar just in time. Shaken by the experience, Mary later reported that she had felt an inexplicable sense of dread and foreboding as they neared the bridge, as if some malevolent force was beckoning her beloved pet to his death.

Another chilling encounter was reported by a local man named James, who claimed to have seen a ghostly figure standing on the bridge late one night. The figure, described as a tall, shadowy presence dressed in old-fashioned clothing, seemed to be staring intently at the spot where the dogs were known to jump. As James watched, the figure slowly faded from view, leaving him with an overwhelming feeling of sadness and despair. This sighting has led some to speculate that the spirit of a long-deceased resident of Overtoun House may be haunting the bridge, their restless soul somehow connected to the tragic canine deaths that continue to occur there.

In addition to the eyewitness accounts of ghostly encounters, numerous paranormal investigations have been conducted at the Overtoun Bridge in an attempt to shed light on the chilling phenomenon. These investigations have employed a variety of techniques and equipment, from electromagnetic field detectors to infrared cameras, in an effort to capture evidence of the enigmatic presence that is believed to haunt the bridge.

One such investigation was led by a team of paranormal researchers from the Scottish Society for Paranormal Research (SSPR). Over the course of several nights, the SSPR team conducted a series of experiments and observations at the bridge, focusing their efforts on the right-hand side where the dog deaths were known to occur. During their investigation, the team reported several instances of unexplained temperature fluctuations and electromagnetic field disturbances, as well as the sensation of being watched by an unseen presence.

Perhaps the most intriguing finding from the SSPR investigation was a series of photographs taken by the team, which appeared to show a faint, mist-like figure hovering near the edge of the bridge. While the images were far from definitive proof of the paranormal, they added to the growing body of evidence that suggested that there may be more to the Overtoun Bridge than meets the eye.

As the mystery of the Overtoun Bridge continues to baffle and captivate both locals and paranormal enthusiasts alike, the tragic canine deaths and chilling encounters with the unknown show no signs of abating. With each new report of a dog leaping to its doom, the bridge's sinister reputation is further cemented, leaving many to wonder what dark secrets may lie hidden beneath its graceful arches and weathered stones.

The Overtoun Bridge serves as a haunting reminder that, even in the most beautiful and tranquil of settings, there may be unseen forces at work that defy our understanding and challenge our perceptions of the world around us. As we continue our exploration of the world's spookiest structures, we must confront the chilling possibility that, in some cases, the stories of haunted bridges may be more than mere folklore and urban legend. Whether the Overtoun Bridge is indeed the site of a supernatural presence or merely the locus of a tragic and inexplicable natural phenomenon, its eerie history and enigmatic allure will continue to draw those who seek to uncover the truth behind its chilling tales.

The Phantom Hitchhiker of Uniondale

Tucked away in the scenic landscape of South Africa's Western Cape province lies the small town of Uniondale. At first glance, this quaint rural settlement seems like an idyllic place to escape the hustle and bustle of modern life. However, beneath the tranquil facade of Uniondale lies a chilling tale of tragedy and the supernatural that has captured the imaginations of locals and visitors alike for decades.

In the heart of this picturesque town stands the Barandas Bridge, a modest structure that spans a serene river surrounded by the rolling hills of the Western Cape's countryside. While the bridge itself may appear unremarkable, it is the setting for one of South Africa's most famous and enduring ghost stories: the tale of the phantom hitchhiker of Uniondale.

The story of the phantom hitchhiker begins on a stormy night in

1968 when a young woman named Maria Roux was tragically killed in a car accident on the Barandas Bridge. Maria was a passenger in the vehicle driven by her fiancé, Gideon, when they lost control of the car and it plunged into the river below. While Gideon managed to escape the wreckage, Maria was not so fortunate, and her body was later found in the mangled remains of the car.

In the years that followed Maria's untimely death, a chilling phenomenon began to emerge at the Barandas Bridge. Numerous motorists driving along the road that crosses the bridge reported encountering a mysterious young woman dressed in white, standing by the side of the road and seemingly in need of assistance. According to the accounts, the young woman would flag down passing vehicles and ask for a ride, claiming that she was trying to get home.

Despite the eerie circumstances of their encounter, many of the drivers who picked up the hitchhiker described her as being quite normal in appearance and demeanour. She would engage in polite conversation and even provide directions to her supposed home. However, as the vehicle approached the bridge, the young woman would suddenly vanish into thin air, leaving her bewildered rescuers with nothing but the chilling memory of their ghostly passenger.

As the stories of the phantom hitchhiker spread, it became apparent that the mysterious young woman bore a striking resemblance to the late Maria Roux, leading many to believe that her restless spirit was haunting the Barandas Bridge in search of a ride home. The legend of the phantom hitchhiker soon became synonymous with the town of Uniondale, and the Barandas Bridge took on a sinister reputation as a place where the living and the dead crossed paths.

Over the years, countless eyewitness accounts have been documented, each one adding to the eerie lore of the phantom hitchhiker. One such account comes from a truck driver named Pieter who had heard the stories of the ghostly hitchhiker but had never given them much credence. That was until one fateful night when he found himself driving along the road near the Barandas Bridge.

As Pieter approached the bridge, he noticed a young woman standing by the side of the road, her white dress illuminated by the headlights of his truck. He slowed down, and the woman asked if he could give her a lift to her home. Pieter agreed, and the young woman climbed into the cab of his truck. They chatted casually as they drove along, and Pieter found himself feeling at ease in her presence.

However, as they neared the Barandas Bridge, the young woman suddenly became agitated and insisted that Pieter stop the truck. Confused, he pulled over and watched in horror as the woman vanished before his very eyes. Shaken by the encounter, Pieter could only come to one conclusion: he had just given a ride to the phantom hitchhiker of Uniondale. This encounter would stay with him for the rest of his life, serving as a chilling reminder of the unexplained events that can occur at the Barandas Bridge.

Another account comes from a woman named Claire, who was driving alone near the bridge late one evening. As she approached the crossing, she noticed a figure in white standing at the side of the road. She pulled over and offered the young woman a ride, believing her to be in distress. As they drove, the hitchhiker appeared to be very quiet and reserved, barely speaking a word.

Feeling increasingly uneasy, Claire glanced in her rearview mirror, only to find that her passenger had vanished. Panicked, she slammed on the brakes and scanned the area, but there was no sign of the mysterious woman. It wasn't until later that Claire discovered the legend of the phantom hitchhiker and realised the gravity of her encounter.

As the years passed, the legend of the phantom hitchhiker continued to grow, drawing curious visitors to Uniondale in search of a ghostly encounter. Locals in the town have mixed feelings about the phenomenon, with some dismissing it as nothing more than a product of overactive imaginations, while others firmly believe that Maria Roux's spirit continues to haunt the Barandas Bridge.

In an attempt to unravel the mystery of the phantom hitchhiker, paranormal investigators have descended upon Uniondale and the Barandas Bridge, seeking to capture evidence of the supernatural. While some have claimed to have recorded strange phenomena, such as unexplained noises and temperature fluctuations, no definitive proof of the phantom hitchhiker's existence has been found.

Despite the lack of concrete evidence, the stories of the phantom hitchhiker continue to captivate those who hear them. Whether or not the ghostly figure truly haunts the Barandas Bridge remains a topic of debate, but one thing is certain: the tale of the phantom hitchhiker has become an enduring part of Uniondale's history, adding an air of mystery and intrigue to the small South African town.

As the sun sets over the rolling hills of the Western Cape, casting shadows across the landscape, the Barandas Bridge stands as a silent witness to the chilling events that have unfolded on its arches. For those who dare to traverse its span in search of the phantom hitchhiker, the bridge offers a glimpse into a world where the veil between the living and the dead grows thin, and the secrets of the past continue to haunt the present.

So, as we continue our journey through the world's spookiest structures, we must ask ourselves: do we have the courage to cross the haunted bridges that lie in our path? Are we prepared to confront the chilling secrets and eerie encounters that await us on the other side? Only time will tell as we delve deeper into the shadows, unearthing the tales of tragedy and the supernatural that lie within the heart of these seemingly ordinary crossings.

La Llorona's Crossing - Albuquerque, New Mexico, USA

The sun dips below the horizon, casting a warm glow across the desert landscape of Albuquerque, New Mexico. As twilight descends, shadows creep along the Rio Grande, their dark tendrils weaving through the sagebrush and cottonwood trees that dot the riverbank. Here, amidst the haunting beauty of the Southwest, lies a bridge shrouded in sorrow and mystery: the Juan Tabo Bridge. Spanning the flowing waters of the Rio Grande, the bridge has become synonymous with the tragic spirit of La Llorona, the weeping woman who is said to haunt its arches and the surrounding area.

To understand the chilling presence that pervades the Juan Tabo Bridge, one must delve into the legend of La Llorona, a tale that has haunted the hearts and minds of the people of New Mexico for generations. The story begins with a young woman named Maria, who lived in a small village near the banks of the Rio

Grande. Known for her enchanting beauty, Maria was the object of desire for many men in the village. Yet, her heart belonged to a wealthy nobleman who had captured her affections.

Their whirlwind romance culminated in a lavish wedding, and the couple was blessed with two children. However, as time passed, the nobleman's attentions began to wane, and he started spending more time away from home, leaving Maria to care for their children alone. With each passing day, her heart grew heavy with sadness, and her once-radiant beauty began to fade.

One fateful evening, as Maria walked along the banks of the Rio Grande with her children, she saw her husband approaching in the distance. Her joy was short-lived, however, when she noticed that he was accompanied by a young, beautiful woman. Consumed by grief and rage, Maria succumbed to a moment of madness and, in a fit of blind fury, pushed her children into the raging waters of the river, where they were swept away by the current.

Realising the gravity of her actions, Maria was filled with despair and spent the remainder of her days wandering the riverbank, weeping for her lost children. When death finally claimed her, her tortured spirit was unable to find rest and continued to haunt the Rio Grande, crying out for her children and searching for them in the dark waters.

This tragic tale has become an enduring part of New Mexican folklore, with countless variations of the story passed down through generations. The spirit of La Llorona has been sighted near bodies of water throughout the Southwest, particularly near bridges that span the Rio Grande. One such crossing, the Juan Tabo Bridge in Albuquerque, has become known as La Llorona's Crossing, due to the numerous encounters with the weeping woman reported in the area.

The Juan Tabo Bridge was built in 1965, providing a vital link between the eastern and western parts of Albuquerque. Though it may appear to be an ordinary concrete and steel structure, those who have ventured across its span at night know that there is something far more sinister lurking beneath the surface.

Over the years, the Juan Tabo Bridge has been the site of numerous reports of paranormal activity, with many claiming to have encountered the spirit of La Llorona. In the darkness, her mournful wails can be heard echoing through the night, a chilling reminder of the sorrow that grips her tortured soul.

One particularly harrowing account comes from a woman named Elena, who was driving across the Juan Tabo Bridge late one night. As she approached the middle of the bridge, she noticed a figure in white standing near the railing, her long hair obscuring her face. Concerned for the woman's safety, Elena slowed her car to a stop and rolled down the window, calling out to ask if she needed help. The figure turned slowly, revealing a face twisted with grief, her eyes streaming with tears. Elena felt a chill run down her spine as the woman began to wail, her voice filled with anguish. Terrified, Elena quickly rolled up her window and sped across the bridge, unable to shake the haunting image of the weeping woman from her mind.

Another encounter with La Llorona at the Juan Tabo Bridge was shared by a group of friends who had ventured to the bridge on a dare. As they walked along the riverbank beneath the bridge, they heard the faint sound of a woman crying. Intrigued, they followed the sound, only to come upon the ghostly figure of La Llorona, her white gown billowing in the wind as she wept by the water's edge. The friends fled in terror, their hearts pounding in their chests as the chilling cries of La Llorona pursued them through the darkness.

These tales, among many others, have cemented the Juan Tabo

Bridge's reputation as a haunted site, with some locals even refusing to cross the bridge after nightfall. The stories of La Llorona's haunting have become so deeply ingrained in Albuquerque's culture that the city has embraced the legend, hosting an annual event known as La Llorona's Night, during which people gather at the bridge to share their own encounters and listen to the chilling wails of the weeping woman.

The legend of La Llorona serves as a cautionary tale, a reminder of the destructive power of jealousy and the enduring nature of grief. As the Juan Tabo Bridge continues to stand as a testament to the tragic spirit that haunts its arches, the people of Albuquerque and the surrounding area are left to ponder the eerie presence that lingers in the shadows.

The Juan Tabo Bridge is not only a haunting reminder of the sorrowful tale of La Llorona, but it also stands as a testament to the enduring power of folklore and the human fascination with the supernatural. As people continue to share their stories of encounters with the weeping woman, the legend of La Llorona's Crossing grows ever more potent, leaving an indelible mark on the hearts and minds of those who dare to cross the haunted bridge.

Whether one views the tales of La Llorona as mere ghost stories or as a genuine supernatural phenomenon, it is undeniable that the Juan Tabo Bridge holds a unique place in the annals of haunted bridges.

The Donkey Lady Bridge - San Antonio, Texas, USA

In the heart of Texas lies the bustling city of San Antonio, a metropolis steeped in history, culture, and a myriad of fascinating stories. Yet, in the shadow of this vibrant city, there exists a tale that sends chills down the spine of even the most hardened sceptic. Just outside the city limits, spanning the murky waters of Elm Creek, is a bridge with a haunting history that has captured the imaginations of both locals and visitors alike. This bridge is none other than the infamous Donkey Lady Bridge, the eerie site of a bizarre and terrifying apparition that has left many shaken to their core.

To understand the haunting of the Donkey Lady Bridge, one must first delve into the dark legend that surrounds it. While the origins of the tale are shrouded in mystery, the most widely accepted version of the story begins with a family living in a small, isolated farmhouse near Elm Creek in the late 19th century. Tragedy struck when a fire ravaged the home, killing the family's two children and leaving the mother horribly disfigured. Her injuries were so severe that her once-human features were distorted beyond recognition, her fingers fused together, and her face elongated and twisted, resembling the grotesque visage of a donkey. Consumed by grief and madness, the woman retreated to the woods surrounding Elm Creek, where she was said to have met her end.

However, death did not bring peace to the tormented soul of the Donkey Lady. Instead, her restless spirit is believed to have taken up residence in the area around the bridge, lying in wait to terrorise those who dare to trespass on her territory.

The bridge itself, constructed in the early 20th century, has become a symbol of the strange and terrifying encounters that have taken place there. The structure's unassuming appearance—a simple concrete slab spanning the narrow creek—belies the sinister presence that is said to lurk in the darkness beneath its arches.

Over the years, numerous eyewitnesses have come forward with chilling accounts of their encounters with the Donkey Lady on or near the bridge. One such story comes from a group of teenagers who ventured to the site on a moonless night, eager to test their courage in the face of the supernatural. As they approached the bridge, they heard the sound of hooves clattering on the concrete, followed by a guttural, inhuman wail that pierced the silence. Gripped by terror, the group fled the scene, swearing never to return.

Another account comes from a man named Jake, who had been fishing in Elm Creek one evening. As the sun dipped below the horizon, he packed up his gear and made his way back to his truck, which was parked near the bridge. As he approached the vehicle, he noticed a hunched figure standing on the bridge, its grotesque features illuminated by the fading light. The creature's eyes locked onto his, and Jake was filled with a sense of dread that seemed to emanate from the very depths of his soul. He raced to his truck and sped away, haunted by the image of the Donkey Lady that lingered in his rearview mirror.

These encounters, among many others, have solidified the Donkey Lady Bridge's reputation as a site of paranormal activity. The bridge has become a popular destination for thrill-seekers and paranormal enthusiasts alike, who flock to the area in the hopes of catching a glimpse of the mysterious and terrifying apparition.

The legend of the Donkey Lady Bridge is not only a testament to the power of folklore and the human fascination with the unknown, but it also serves as a chilling reminder of the darker side of our shared human experience. As the bridge continues to draw the curious and the brave, the stories of encounters with the Donkey Lady only grow more numerous, adding to the eerie legacy of this haunted crossing.

In addition to the numerous eyewitness accounts of the Donkey Lady, there are also reports of strange occurrences and inexplicable phenomena that seem to defy rational explanation. Some visitors to the bridge have claimed to hear the sound of hooves echoing through the night, accompanied by an otherworldly wailing that sends shivers down their spines. Others have described feeling a sudden drop in temperature or an oppressive, malevolent presence that seems to hang in the air around the bridge.

One particularly chilling account comes from a woman named Marisol, who had been driving along the rural road leading to the bridge late one night. As she approached the crossing, her car suddenly stalled, leaving her stranded in the darkness. Desperate to get her vehicle running again, she stepped out into the night and began to investigate the issue. As she worked, she couldn't shake the feeling that she was being watched. Glancing up, she saw the twisted figure of the Donkey Lady standing on the bridge, her grotesque face illuminated by the moonlight. Panicking, Marisol managed to get her car started and quickly drove away, forever haunted by the memory of that fateful encounter.

These stories, along with countless others, have contributed to the enduring allure of the Donkey Lady Bridge. As the legend continues to grow, so too does the bridge's infamy, attracting visitors from far and wide in search of a chilling brush with the supernatural. Whether one views these tales as mere campfire stories or as genuine paranormal phenomena, the Donkey Lady Bridge remains a fascinating and terrifying fixture in the annals of haunted bridges.

As the sun sets over the Texan landscape and darkness descends upon the bridge, the air grows heavy with anticipation, and a sense of unease settles over the surrounding area. Will the Donkey Lady make her presence known once more? Or will her spirit rest, if only for a night, in the murky depths of Elm Creek? Only the brave—or the foolish—dare to venture to the bridge after nightfall, risking a chilling encounter with the tormented soul that is said to dwell there.

As the legend of the Donkey Lady Bridge continues to capture the imaginations of those who hear it, the bridge stands as a testament to the enduring power of folklore and the human fascination with the supernatural. The tales of terror and sorrow that surround the bridge serve as both a cautionary tale and an irresistible invitation, beckoning the curious and the brave to experience the chilling embrace of the Donkey Lady for themselves. Will you be among them? Only time will tell.

Clifton Suspension Bridge - Bristol, England

Spanning the Avon Gorge in Bristol, England, the Clifton Suspension Bridge has long been an iconic symbol of the city's rich history and engineering prowess. Designed by the legendary Isambard Kingdom Brunel, this majestic bridge has stood proudly since its completion in 1864, a testament to the ingenuity and vision of its creator. But beneath its striking beauty lies a darker legacy, one of eerie occurrences and ghostly sightings that have earned the bridge a place in the annals of haunted bridges around the world.

The history of the Clifton Suspension Bridge dates back to the early 19th century, when the need for a crossing over the Avon Gorge became increasingly evident. The gorge's steep cliffs and the powerful currents of the River Avon made the construction of a traditional bridge all but impossible, prompting the search for an innovative solution. In 1830, the Clifton Suspension

Bridge Trust held a competition to design a new bridge that could span the formidable gorge. Brunel, then a young engineer with a passion for pushing the boundaries of what was possible, submitted a daring design that would ultimately win the competition and shape the future of the city.

Construction on the bridge began in 1831, but progress was slow due to a lack of funds and the many technical challenges posed by the site. It was not until 1864, after Brunel's death, that the bridge was finally completed, standing as a lasting tribute to his genius and perseverance. Today, the Clifton Suspension Bridge remains an active crossing for pedestrians and vehicles alike, as well as a popular tourist attraction that draws visitors from around the world.

But for all its architectural splendour, the Clifton Suspension Bridge harbours a darker side, one that has given rise to chilling tales of ghostly apparitions and eerie phenomena. Over the years, the bridge has been the site of numerous suicides, with some estimates suggesting that more than 500 people have taken their own lives by leaping from its lofty heights. This tragic legacy has given rise to countless stories of spectral figures and strange occurrences, as the restless spirits of the departed are said to linger in the shadows of the bridge.

One of the most well-known ghost stories associated with the Clifton Suspension Bridge concerns the spirit of a young woman named Sarah Ann Henley, who is said to haunt the bridge to this day. In 1885, Sarah, a 22-year-old barmaid, was engaged to be married, but her fiancé broke off the engagement just days before the wedding. Distraught, she decided to end her life by jumping from the bridge. However, fate had other plans, and as she plummeted towards the water below, her billowing skirts caught the wind, slowing her descent and allowing her to survive the fall. Sarah went on to live a long life, eventually passing away at the age of 85.

Despite her remarkable survival, many believe that Sarah's spirit never left the bridge. Over the years, numerous witnesses have reported seeing a ghostly figure in Victorian dress near the spot where Sarah made her fateful leap. Some have even claimed to see the apparition floating in mid-air, as though suspended by an unseen force, before vanishing without a trace. These sightings have led many to believe that Sarah's spirit continues to haunt the bridge, a tragic reminder of the heartbreak and despair that drove her to the brink of suicide.

Another chilling tale associated with the Clifton Suspension Bridge involves a mysterious figure known as the Man in Black.

This spectral figure has been sighted on numerous occasions, often by motorists driving across the bridge late at night. According to eyewitness accounts, the Man in Black appears suddenly in the road, forcing drivers to swerve to avoid hitting him. As they regain control of their vehicles and glance back, the figure has vanished, leaving no trace of his presence. The identity of the Man in Black remains a mystery, but some speculate that he may be the spirit of a man who met a tragic end on the bridge, perhaps another victim of the dark allure that has led so many to take their own lives.

Beyond these specific accounts, there have been numerous other reports of strange occurrences and ghostly sightings on and around the Clifton Suspension Bridge. Witnesses have described hearing eerie cries echoing through the gorge late at night, as if the wind itself carries the tormented screams of the bridge's many lost souls. Others have reported feeling sudden cold spots or an inexplicable sense of dread as they walk across the bridge, only for these sensations to dissipate as they leave the area.

The haunted history of the Clifton Suspension Bridge has attracted the attention of paranormal investigators, who have sought to uncover the truth behind these ghostly encounters. While some maintain that the bridge's eerie reputation can be attributed to natural phenomena, such as the eerie acoustics of the gorge or the play of shadows on the bridge's imposing structure, others believe that the sheer number and consistency of the reported sightings suggest that something more sinister may be at work.

In one notable investigation, a team of paranormal researchers spent the night on the bridge, armed with an array of equipment designed to detect the presence of supernatural activity. While they did not encounter any full-bodied apparitions, they did record several instances of unexplained cold spots and fluctuations in the ambient temperature, as well as a number of strange sounds that could not be easily explained. While these findings may not provide definitive proof of the bridge's haunted status, they do lend credence to the notion that something otherworldly may be lurking in the shadows of this iconic structure.

As the Clifton Suspension Bridge continues to serve as a vital link between the two halves of Bristol, it also remains a source of fascination and fear for those who have encountered its ghostly residents. The stories of Sarah Ann Henley, the Man in Black, and countless others who have met their untimely end on the bridge serve as a chilling reminder of the darker side of human nature and the enduring allure of the supernatural.

The Crying Bridge of Malaysia - Penang, Malaysia

In the heart of Penang, Malaysia, lies a bridge shrouded in tragedy and haunted by the echoes of a sorrowful past. Known as the Crying Bridge of Malaysia, the Pekan Bridge has long been the subject of chilling tales and supernatural events. As we delve into the dark history and eerie occurrences linked to this haunted structure, we are reminded that, while bridges are meant to connect people and places, they can also serve as a conduit for the supernatural and the unknown.

The Pekan Bridge, located in the bustling city of Penang, was originally built in the 1960s as part of a broader effort to modernise the area's infrastructure and promote economic growth. Spanning the Sungai Juru River, the bridge was designed to facilitate the movement of goods and people between the two sides of the river, fostering connections and opportunities for the local community. Over the years, the bridge has undergone several renovations and expansions to keep pace with the ever-growing demands of the region.

However, unbeknownst to many, the Pekan Bridge has a tragic history that predates its construction. In the early 20th century, the area surrounding the bridge was the site of a terrible accident that left dozens dead and many more injured. According to local lore, a train carrying passengers and cargo derailed near the river, plummeting into the waters below. The exact cause of the accident remains a mystery, but many believe that the spirits of those who perished in the crash still haunt the bridge to this day.

The most chilling aspect of the Pekan Bridge's haunted history is the phenomenon for which it is named: the eerie cries and wails that are said to emanate from the structure late at night. Many who have ventured across the bridge after dark have reported hearing these mournful sounds, as if the souls of the victims are still trapped beneath the water, their cries for help echoing through the still night air.

One local resident, a man named Aziz, shared his experience of crossing the Pekan Bridge late one night while returning home from work. As he made his way across the bridge, he began to hear faint cries and wails, growing louder and more insistent as he continued. At first, he believed it to be the sound of children playing near the river, but as he looked around, he realised there was no one in sight. The cries seemed to surround him, growing more intense with each step, until he could no longer bear the overwhelming sadness and fear that gripped him. He fled the bridge, convinced that the spirits of the dead had made their presence known.

In addition to the chilling cries that give the Pekan Bridge its nickname, there have been numerous reports of other paranormal occurrences and ghostly sightings on and around the structure. Some have claimed to see shadowy figures lurking near the water's edge, while others have experienced sudden cold spots or inexplicable feelings of dread as they cross the bridge.

One particularly harrowing account comes from a woman named Lina, who was driving across the bridge with her family late one night. As they approached the midpoint of the bridge, Lina noticed a figure standing at the edge of the road, seemingly staring into the water below. Concerned for the individual's safety, she slowed down, only to realise that the figure appeared to be a woman dressed in traditional Malay attire, her long hair and flowing garments seemingly untouched by the wind. As Lina drew closer, the woman turned to face her, revealing a face contorted with anguish and despair. Lina quickly drove away, her heart pounding, convinced that she had encountered one of the restless spirits said to haunt the bridge.

Over the years, the tales of the Crying Bridge of Malaysia have piqued the interest of paranormal investigators, who have travelled to Penang in search of answers to the eerie occurrences and ghostly sightings. Many have come equipped with an array of devices designed to detect and document supernatural activity, hoping to capture evidence of the spirits that are believed to haunt the bridge.

In one notable investigation, a team of paranormal researchers spent several nights on and around the Pekan Bridge, attempting to communicate with the spirits and record any signs of their presence. During their time on the bridge, they experienced several instances of unexplained cold spots, sudden drops in temperature, and fluctuations in the electromagnetic field. While they did not capture any visual evidence of full-bodied apparitions, they did record a number of strange sounds, including faint cries and wails that seemed to defy any natural explanation.

These findings, while not definitive, lend credence to the local legends surrounding the Pekan Bridge and suggest that there may indeed be something otherworldly at play. As with many haunted bridges around the world, the tales of the Crying Bridge of Malaysia serve as a chilling reminder of the tragedies that have unfolded in these seemingly ordinary places and the enduring allure of the supernatural.

The haunted Pekan Bridge continues to serve as a vital connection for the people of Penang, facilitating the movement of goods and people across the Sungai Juru River. However, for those who have encountered the eerie cries and ghostly apparitions that are said to haunt the bridge, it remains a place of mystery and fear.

The Ghostly Battle of Stoney Creek - Stoney Creek, Ontario, Canada

In the quiet town of Stoney Creek, Ontario, Canada, a bridge shrouded in supernatural lore spans the landscape, its storied past etched in the memories of both the living and the dead. The Battlefield Park Bridge, a seemingly ordinary structure, serves as the backdrop for the ghostly Battle of Stoney Creek, where spectral soldiers continue to fight, their spirits forever tethered to this haunted site. As we delve into the chilling tales and eerie encounters surrounding the Battlefield Park Bridge, we are reminded that some battles, even after centuries have passed, are never truly over.

The history of the Battlefield Park Bridge is intrinsically tied to a significant event in Canadian history: the Battle of Stoney Creek.

Fought on June 6, 1813, during the War of 1812, this pivotal confrontation between British and American forces resulted in a decisive British victory that ultimately helped to shape the course of the war. The battlefield, now a historic site and park, serves as a testament to the bravery and sacrifice of the soldiers who fought and died there.

The Battlefield Park Bridge, built in the early 20th century, connects the main area of the park with the historic Gage House, the former residence of the Gage family who played a significant role in the battle. The bridge, while not an original feature of the battlefield, has become an integral part of the park's landscape and a focal point for the chilling tales and supernatural encounters that have come to define the area.

Visitors to the Battlefield Park Bridge have reported a variety of ghostly sightings and unexplained phenomena, many of which are believed to be linked to the spirits of the soldiers who perished during the Battle of Stoney Creek. Among the most common experiences are sightings of spectral soldiers, clad in the uniforms of the British and American forces, locked in an eternal struggle on the bridge and the surrounding parkland. These ghostly warriors, their faces etched with determination and despair, appear to be unaware of the passage of time, their final moments of battle replayed again and again in a haunting display of supernatural unrest.

One eyewitness, a local historian named Thomas, shared his harrowing encounter with the ghostly soldiers of the Battlefield Park Bridge. Late one evening, while walking through the park, Thomas approached the bridge and suddenly found himself enveloped in a dense fog that seemed to appear out of nowhere. As he continued across the bridge, he was startled to see the faint outlines of soldiers emerging from the mist, their ghostly forms engaged in a fierce and desperate battle. The clash of swords and the cries of the fallen filled the air, the spectral scene unfolding before him in a haunting tableau of war and death. As quickly as it had begun, the ghostly battle dissipated, leaving Thomas shaken and convinced that he had witnessed the lingering spirits of the Battle of Stoney Creek.

In addition to the ghostly soldiers, visitors to the Battlefield Park Bridge have reported other unexplained phenomena, including eerie lights that seem to dance across the bridge late at night, disembodied voices echoing through the park, and sudden cold spots that envelop unsuspecting passersby. These paranormal experiences have led many to believe that the Battlefield Park Bridge is not only a site of historic significance but also a nexus of supernatural activity.

The ghostly Battle of Stoney Creek has drawn the attention of paranormal investigators, eager to explore the haunted Battlefield Park Bridge and attempt to document the supernatural phenomena that have become synonymous with the site. In one notable investigation, a team of paranormal researchers spent several nights at the bridge and the surrounding park, armed with an array of equipment designed to detect and record the presence of supernatural activity.

During their time at the Battlefield Park Bridge, the investigators captured several instances of unexplained phenomena, including temperature fluctuations, electromagnetic field disturbances, and even faint EVP (Electronic Voice Phenomena) recordings that seemed to suggest the presence of disembodied voices. While no definitive visual evidence of full-bodied apparitions was obtained, the findings of the investigation lend credence to the stories of ghostly soldiers and supernatural activity at the Battlefield Park Bridge.

The ghostly Battle of Stoney Creek and the haunted Battlefield Park Bridge serve as poignant reminders of the sacrifices made by the soldiers who fought and died on this hallowed ground.

The bridge, once a simple structure connecting two points within the park, has taken on a life of its own, its haunting tales and eerie encounters transforming it into an enigmatic and chilling landmark.

The stories and experiences shared by visitors to the Battlefield Park Bridge paint a vivid picture of a site where history and the supernatural collide, the spirits of fallen soldiers forever bound to the place of their final battle. As we continue our exploration of the world's spookiest structures in "Haunted Bridges: Eerie Encounters from The World's Spookiest Structures," we are reminded that some places, even centuries after their tragic histories have unfolded, continue to resonate with an otherworldly energy that cannot be easily explained.

The Battlefield Park Bridge and the ghostly Battle of Stoney Creek serve as a testament to the enduring power of the supernatural and the haunted bridges that captivate our imaginations. As we delve deeper into the eerie encounters and chilling tales that define these mysterious structures, we are left to wonder: what other ghostly secrets lie hidden within the shadows of the world's most haunted bridges?

El Muerto of Texas - Refugio, Texas, USA

The great state of Texas is no stranger to tales of the supernatural and paranormal. Ghostly encounters and eerie legends have been woven into the fabric of its history, forming an integral part of its cultural identity. In Refugio, a small town in the heart of southern Texas, one such tale stands out - the chilling legend of El Muerto, the headless horseman who is said to haunt the Refugio River Bridge.

The Refugio River Bridge, a seemingly unassuming structure, spans the serene waters of the Refugio River. Built in the early 20th century, the bridge was designed to connect the town of Refugio to the surrounding communities and facilitate trade and transportation. While the history of the bridge itself is relatively mundane, the area around Refugio has a much darker and more mysterious past.

In the early 1800s, during the tumultuous period of the Texas Revolution, the region around Refugio was a battleground for the fierce conflict between Mexican forces and Texan revolutionaries. It was during this time that the legend of El Muerto, the headless horseman, was born.

As the story goes, a Mexican general named Vidal was tasked with the responsibility of quelling Texan resistance in the area. To strike fear into the hearts of his enemies, General Vidal employed a ruthless tactic: he captured a Texan revolutionary, decapitated him, and tied his lifeless body to a wild mustang. The general then fastened the severed head to the saddle, creating a gruesome and terrifying spectacle. This horrifying sight was intended to serve as a warning to those who dared to defy Mexican rule.

However, as legend has it, the plan backfired. The headless corpse, known as El Muerto, began to appear on moonlit nights, riding across the plains and terrorising both Mexican soldiers and Texan revolutionaries alike. The mustang, seemingly unable to escape the ghostly rider, was said to have become a phantom itself, forever trapped in a state of restless torment.

In the years that followed, El Muerto continued to be spotted by travellers and locals in the area surrounding Refugio. The grisly spectre seemed to be drawn to the bridge that now spans the Refugio River, making it a focal point for supernatural activity. Over time, the bridge itself became inextricably linked to the legend of the headless horseman.

Today, the Refugio River Bridge is known as one of the most haunted bridges in the world. Visitors and locals alike have reported sightings of the ghostly rider, his decapitated head still swinging from the saddle as he rides his spectral steed across the bridge. Eyewitness accounts describe a palpable sense of dread and unease that seems to emanate from the bridge, with some even claiming to have heard the anguished cries of El Muerto's phantom horse.

One particularly chilling account comes from a local rancher who, in the late 1970s, was driving his cattle across the Refugio River Bridge. The rancher claims that as he approached the bridge, the temperature suddenly dropped, and an overwhelming feeling of dread washed over him. As he pressed on, he caught sight of a shadowy figure emerging from the darkness. It was El Muerto, his headless body swaying in the saddle as he charged across the bridge. The rancher, paralyzed with fear, could only watch in horror as the spectral rider disappeared into the night.

Another eyewitness, a group of teenagers who had ventured to the bridge late one night in the early 1990s, recalled a similarly harrowing encounter. As they approached the Refugio River Bridge, the group began to feel an inexplicable sense of unease. Hesitant but determined to face their fears, they continued on to the bridge. As they reached the centre of the structure, they were suddenly enveloped by a thick, unnatural fog. Emerging from the mist, they saw the ghostly figure of El Muerto and his spectral steed. The headless rider charged towards them, causing the group to flee in terror back to the safety of their car.

These chilling stories are just a few of the many accounts of paranormal activity at the Refugio River Bridge. The legend of El Muerto, the headless horseman, has become ingrained in the folklore of the area, and the bridge itself has become a site of eerie fascination for ghost hunters and thrill-seekers alike.

But what is it about this unassuming bridge that has drawn the spirit of El Muerto to it? Some speculate that the Refugio River Bridge stands on a ley line, a supposed alignment of geographical sites with spiritual significance, which could serve as a conduit for supernatural energy. Others believe that the bridge may have been built on the site of a long-forgotten battlefield or burial ground from the time of the Texas Revolution, imbuing it with a deep sense of residual anguish and unrest.

Whatever the cause, the haunting of the Refugio River Bridge has become an enduring piece of local legend, with generations of residents and visitors alike finding themselves captivated by the chilling tale of El Muerto. As the legend has grown and evolved over the years, so too has the sense of mystery that surrounds the bridge, making it a must-visit destination for those seeking a taste of the supernatural.

In conclusion, the haunting of the Refugio River Bridge is a fascinating and chilling example of the enduring power of local folklore and legend. The story of El Muerto, the headless horseman, has captivated the imaginations of countless individuals, making the bridge a site of eerie fascination and a testament to the dark and mysterious history of the area.

The Vanishing Lady of Barmby Moor - Barmby Moor, England

England is a land steeped in history, folklore, and ghostly tales. From the fog-shrouded streets of Victorian London to the haunted castles that dot the countryside, supernatural encounters have long been a part of the nation's rich tapestry of storytelling. One such tale comes from the small village of Barmby Moor, nestled in the heart of East Riding of Yorkshire. Here, the Barmby Moor Bridge, an unassuming stone structure that spans the picturesque River Derwent, has become the centre of a chilling legend: the story of the Vanishing Lady.

Constructed in the early 19th century, the Barmby Moor Bridge was built to facilitate transportation and commerce between Barmby Moor and the neighbouring villages. The bridge, with its elegant arches and weathered stone, has stood the test of time, serving as a silent witness to the countless lives that have traversed its length. However, beneath its serene facade lies a dark and mysterious tale, one that has haunted the residents of Barmby Moor for generations.

The legend of the Vanishing Lady dates back to the mid-1800s, during a period of great social upheaval and change in England. The Industrial Revolution was in full swing, and the quiet rural village of Barmby Moor found itself struggling to adapt to the rapidly shifting landscape. It was during this tumultuous time that a young woman named Amelia was betrothed to a wealthy landowner from a neighbouring village. Despite her misgivings, Amelia consented to the marriage, believing it to be the best course of action for her family's financial security.

On the eve of her wedding day, Amelia, unable to bear the thought of a loveless marriage, decided to flee her home and seek refuge with a distant relative in a nearby village. Clad in her wedding gown, she set off under the cover of darkness, making her way towards the Barmby Moor Bridge. As she crossed the bridge, tragedy struck. Amelia, weighed down by her heavy dress, lost her footing and fell into the icy waters of the River Derwent. Despite her desperate struggle, the current proved too strong, and she was swept away to her untimely demise.

In the years that followed, strange occurrences began to be reported at the Barmby Moor Bridge. Travellers crossing the bridge late at night would catch glimpses of a ghostly figure, clad in white, standing at the edge of the structure. As they approached, the figure would vanish, leaving behind nothing but an eerie sense of sadness and loss. This spectral apparition soon became known as the Vanishing Lady, and her tragic tale became an enduring part of local folklore.

Numerous eyewitness accounts of encounters with the Vanishing Lady have been recorded over the years. One particularly chilling account comes from a local farmer named Thomas, who in the early 1900s was returning home from a neighbouring village late one evening. As he approached the Barmby Moor Bridge, he noticed a figure standing at the edge of the bridge, her white dress billowing in the wind. Believing it to be a woman in distress, Thomas called out to her, but as he drew closer, the figure simply vanished before his eyes.

Another encounter, this time from the 1950s, was reported by a group of young friends who had been enjoying an evening at the local pub. As they crossed the bridge on their way home, they too spotted the figure of a woman in white. Intrigued and emboldened by their youthful bravado, they approached the figure, only to have her disappear right before their eyes. The group, shaken by the experience, hurriedly continued on their way, never to forget the eerie encounter with the Vanishing Lady.

The legend of the Vanishing Lady has not only endured but grown over time, with countless more encounters reported throughout the years. Some believe that Amelia's restless spirit is unable to move on due to the tragic nature of her death, while others speculate that her presence may be connected to a hidden family secret or long-buried scandal. Whatever the reason, the haunting of the Barmby Moor Bridge has become an integral part of the village's history and identity.

In recent years, paranormal investigators and ghost hunters have been drawn to the bridge, eager to uncover the truth behind the legend of the Vanishing Lady. While many have captured unexplained phenomena on film, such as orbs of light and unaccountable mists, definitive proof of Amelia's spirit remains elusive. However, the numerous eyewitness accounts and the enduring nature of the tale have left many convinced that the Vanishing Lady is more than just a local myth.

The Barmby Moor Bridge, with its seemingly ordinary appearance and serene surroundings, may appear an unlikely setting for a haunting, but the legend of the Vanishing Lady serves as a stark reminder of the powerful connection between history, folklore, and the supernatural. As with many haunted bridges around the world, the Barmby Moor Bridge is a testament to the enduring power of storytelling and the human fascination with the unknown.

As we continue our exploration of haunted bridges and their eerie encounters, the story of the Vanishing Lady of Barmby Moor stands out as a haunting and poignant example of love, loss, and tragedy. The bridge, once a symbol of progress and connectivity, now serves as a sombre reminder of the past and a chilling destination for those seeking to experience the supernatural. The Vanishing Lady may remain an enigma, but her story continues to captivate and intrigue all who cross the Barmby Moor Bridge.

The Haunted Bridge of Avignon - Avignon, France

In the heart of southern France lies the historic city of Avignon, a place steeped in history, art, and culture. Encircled by ancient ramparts and perched on the banks of the Rhône River, the city has long been a center of trade, religion, and power. Spanning the Rhône is the Pont d'Avignon, or the Avignon Bridge, a structure that has become as famous for its haunting legends and paranormal activity as it has for its architectural beauty and historical significance.

Constructed in the 12th century, the Pont d'Avignon, originally known as the Pont Saint-Bénézet, was named after the young shepherd who, according to legend, was instructed by divine intervention to build a bridge across the Rhône. Under Bénézet's guidance, the bridge was completed in the early 1180s, stretching nearly a kilometre across the river and featuring 22 elegant arches. The structure became a vital link between

Avignon and the surrounding regions, facilitating trade and pilgrimage routes, and even housing a small chapel dedicated to Saint Nicholas, the patron saint of travellers.

However, the Pont d'Avignon's storied past has also been marred by tragedy and devastation. Over the centuries, the bridge has been battered and partially destroyed by numerous floods, leaving only four of its original arches standing today. The once grand structure, now a fragment of its former self, seems to bear the weight of its tumultuous history, and with it, an eerie atmosphere that has given rise to countless tales of spectral sightings and paranormal activity.

The haunting of the Pont d'Avignon is said to have begun in the 17th century when a young woman named Isabelle fell in love with a soldier stationed in the city. Their love blossomed against the backdrop of the bridge, where they would often meet in secret, hidden in the shadows of its arches. Tragically, their love was not meant to be, as the soldier was soon called to the front lines, never to return. Heartbroken and unable to cope with her loss, Isabelle took her own life by leaping from the highest point of the bridge into the churning waters below.

Since that fateful day, many have claimed to see Isabelle's ghost wandering the bridge at night, forever searching for her lost love. Her spectral figure, clad in a flowing white gown, is said to glide gracefully across the remaining arches, her mournful gaze fixed on the dark waters of the Rhône. Those who have encountered Isabelle's spirit describe an overwhelming sense of sadness that seems to emanate from her ethereal form, as if her grief has become an inextricable part of the bridge itself.

In addition to the legend of Isabelle, other eerie encounters have been reported at the Pont d'Avignon, further fueling its reputation as a haunted bridge. Some claim to have seen mysterious shadows darting between the arches or heard disembodied footsteps echoing through the night. Others have reported strange, unexplainable phenomena such as sudden drops in temperature and the feeling of being watched by an unseen presence.

One particularly chilling eyewitness account comes from a group of tourists visiting the bridge at dusk. As they strolled along the structure, they noticed a figure standing near the edge of one of the arches, staring intently at the water below. Believing it to be a fellow visitor, they called out to the figure, only to watch in horror as it dissolved into thin air right before their eyes.

The haunting of the Pont d'Avignon has become an enduring part of the bridge's history and a source of fascination for both locals and visitors alike. As the sun sets and darkness descends upon the city, the bridge takes on a more sinister and mysterious atmosphere, as if the very air is charged with the energies of the past.

The legends and ghostly sightings surrounding the Pont d'Avignon have attracted the attention of paranormal investigators, eager to uncover the truth behind the eerie encounters. These investigators have used a range of techniques, from traditional spiritual methods to cutting-edge technology, in an attempt to document the spectral activity on the bridge. While some have captured unexplained phenomena, such as sudden temperature fluctuations, unaccountable mists, and orbs of light, definitive proof of the bridge's haunting remains elusive.

One theory that has been suggested to explain the high number of paranormal occurrences on the Pont d'Avignon is the concept of "stone tape theory." This hypothesis posits that certain materials, such as stone, can absorb and store emotional energy, particularly in times of intense emotion or tragedy. When the conditions are right, this energy can be released and manifest as a supernatural event or apparition. Given the bridge's tumultuous past and its association with heartbreak, loss, and devastation, it is not difficult to imagine how such a theory could be applied to the haunting of the Pont d'Avignon.

Regardless of the veracity of the ghostly tales, the Pont d'Avignon remains a place of historical and cultural significance in the city of Avignon. The bridge's partial ruins serve as a tangible reminder of the passage of time and the power of nature, while its legends and spectral sightings add an air of mystery and intrigue to the city's rich tapestry of stories.

As we continue our exploration of the world's haunted bridges, the Pont d'Avignon stands out as an example of how the past can linger in the present, both in a physical and metaphysical sense. The bridge's enduring legends and eerie encounters not only capture the imagination of those who visit but also serve as a testament to the deep and lasting connection between history, folklore, and the supernatural.

The Ghosts of Sydney Harbour Bridge - Sydney, Australia

Sydney Harbour Bridge, affectionately known as the "Coathanger" due to its distinctive arch shape, is an iconic landmark and one of the most famous bridges in the world. Connecting the central business district of Sydney with the North Shore, the bridge is a symbol of the city's progress and a testament to human ingenuity. Completed in 1932, the massive steel structure has become an essential part of Sydney's skyline, attracting tourists from all over the world who come to marvel at its impressive scale and design.

However, beyond the stunning architecture and the breathtaking views, the Sydney Harbour Bridge has a darker and more mysterious side. Over the years, numerous tales of supernatural occurrences and ghostly residents have emerged, suggesting that the bridge may be haunted by spirits from its past. In this chapter, we will delve into the eerie tales and legends surrounding the Sydney Harbour Bridge, exploring the history of the bridge, its hauntings, and the eyewitness accounts of those who have encountered the ghosts that are said to reside there.

The construction of the Sydney Harbour Bridge was a monumental undertaking that spanned nearly a decade. Over 1,400 workers toiled on the project, labouring in dangerous conditions to create the world's largest single-arch bridge at the time. The bridge's construction was not without its tragedies; at least 16 workers lost their lives in accidents during the project, and many more were injured. It is perhaps these tragic deaths, as well as the countless emotions and energies exerted in the bridge's creation, that have given rise to the supernatural phenomena reported on and around the structure.

One of the most famous ghost stories associated with the Sydney Harbour Bridge involves the spirit of a young girl who is said to haunt the area near the southern pylon. According to local legend, the girl, whose name is believed to be Emily, fell to her death from the bridge in the 1930s. Since then, her ghost has been spotted by numerous witnesses, often appearing as a sad, pale figure in a white dress. Emily's spirit is said to be particularly active during the early hours of the morning and has been known to approach unsuspecting motorists who are crossing the bridge. Some have reported seeing her standing at the edge of the bridge, gazing down into the waters of the harbour below, while others claim to have heard her melancholy cries carried on the wind.

Another ghostly resident of the Sydney Harbour Bridge is the spirit of a worker who lost his life during the bridge's construction. Known as the "Phantom Workman," this ghost has been seen by numerous witnesses, often appearing as a shadowy figure dressed in old-fashioned work clothes. The Phantom Workman is said to haunt the area around the bridge's northern pylon, where he can sometimes be seen climbing the steel girders or walking along the arch. Some believe that the spirit is that of a worker named Samuel, who fell to his death while working on the bridge in the 1920s. Samuel's ghost is said to be friendly and protective, and there have even been reports of the spirit warning people away from dangerous areas on the bridge.

In addition to the ghostly residents of the Sydney Harbour Bridge, there have been several accounts of unexplained phenomena occurring on the structure. One particularly chilling story involves a group of friends who were walking across the bridge late one night. As they approached the centre of the span, they noticed a mysterious figure standing by the railing, seemingly staring out at the harbour. The figure appeared to be wearing a long coat and a wide-brimmed hat, and as the group drew closer, they could see that the figure was transparent and ethereal. Suddenly, the figure turned to face them, and the friends were struck by an overwhelming sense of dread. Without warning, the apparition vanished into thin air, leaving the group shaken and unsettled by their ghostly encounter.

There have also been reports of unexplained cold spots on the bridge, with some visitors claiming to have experienced sudden drops in temperature as they walked across the span. These cold spots are often accompanied by a sense of unease and the feeling of being watched, causing many to speculate that they are the result of paranormal activity. Some paranormal investigators believe that the cold spots may be evidence of the spirits of those who died during the bridge's construction, their energy still lingering on the structure.

The Sydney Harbour Bridge has also been the site of numerous unexplained and seemingly paranormal events. One such incident occurred in the early 2000s when a local photographer captured a series of images of the bridge at night. Upon examining the photographs, the photographer noticed a mysterious figure standing on one of the bridge's beams, high above the water. The figure appeared to be dressed in old-fashioned work clothes and was staring directly at the camera. Although the photographer was certain that no one had been on the bridge at the time the photos were taken, they could find no rational explanation for the apparition. The images have since become the subject of much debate and speculation, with many believing they show the spirit of the Phantom Workman.

Eyewitness accounts of ghostly encounters on the Sydney Harbour Bridge continue to be reported to this day, fueling the legend of the bridge's haunted reputation. One such account comes from a local resident named Emma, who experienced a chilling encounter while walking across the bridge late one night. As she made her way across the span, Emma noticed a figure standing by the railing, appearing to stare out at the harbour. As she drew closer, Emma realised that the figure was that of a young girl, dressed in a white dress and with long, flowing hair. The girl seemed to be crying, and as Emma approached her, she felt an overwhelming sense of sadness and despair. Suddenly, the girl turned to face Emma, revealing a tear-streaked face and empty, hollow eyes. Just as quickly as she had appeared, the girl vanished into the night, leaving Emma shaken and convinced that she had encountered the spirit of Emily.

The haunting tales and legends of the Sydney Harbour Bridge serve as a reminder of the bridge's tragic past and the lives lost during its construction. Whether the ghostly residents are the spirits of those who died on the bridge or merely figments of the imagination, the stories of the Ghosts of Sydney Harbour Bridge continue to captivate and terrify those who dare to cross its haunted span. As Sydney's iconic landmark continues to stand as a symbol of progress and human achievement, the eerie encounters and paranormal activity that surround it ensure that the bridge's darker side will never be forgotten.

The Weeping Woman of Malabadi Bridge - Silvan, Turkey

In the southeastern region of Turkey, where the Tigris River meanders through the ancient landscape, the Malabadi Bridge stands as a testament to the architectural prowess of those who built it. Constructed in the 12th century during the Artuqid Dynasty, the Malabadi Bridge was once a vital link along the Silk Road, facilitating trade and cultural exchange between the East and the West. This impressive stone structure spans the river with a single pointed arch, a true marvel of engineering for its time. But hidden within the shadows of the bridge's ancient stones lies a heart-wrenching tale of love, betrayal, and eternal sorrow – the story of the Weeping Woman of Malabadi Bridge.

The story of the Weeping Woman dates back to the time when

the Malabadi Bridge was being constructed. As the tale goes, a young and beautiful woman named Leyla lived in a village near the construction site. Leyla was deeply in love with a local stonemason named Hassan, who was working on the construction of the bridge. They often met by the river, stealing moments of happiness amid the chaos and toil of the project.

Unbeknownst to the couple, their love was not meant to be. A wealthy and powerful man named Selim had set his sights on Leyla and was determined to make her his bride. Selim was a ruthless man, and he would stop at nothing to get what he wanted. When he learned of Leyla's love for Hassan, he grew consumed with jealousy and rage. He devised a wicked plan to separate the lovers and claim Leyla as his own.

Selim approached the chief architect of the bridge, an old and wise man named Ismail, and made a sinister proposition. In exchange for a large sum of money, Ismail was to ensure that the bridge would collapse, killing Hassan and the other workers in the process. With no other choice but to comply, Ismail reluctantly agreed to Selim's demand.

That fateful night, as the workers slept, Ismail sabotaged the bridge. The following day, as the workers crossed the bridge, it suddenly gave way, plunging them into the raging waters of the Tigris River. Hassan and many others perished in the disaster.

Leyla was devastated by the loss of her beloved Hassan. When Selim came to claim her as his bride, she refused to marry him, sensing his evil intentions. Enraged, Selim locked Leyla in a tower near the river, where she was forced to watch as the bridge was rebuilt, a constant reminder of the tragedy that had befallen her.

As the years passed, Leyla's heartbreak turned into despair, and she spent her days weeping for her lost love. The villagers would often hear her mournful cries echoing through the night, her tears falling like rain upon the river below. Eventually, her grief consumed her, and she died in the tower, her soul forever bound to the bridge and the sorrow it held.

To this day, locals and visitors alike have reported sightings of the Weeping Woman at the Malabadi Bridge. She is said to appear on moonlit nights, her ethereal form drifting along the riverbank, her cries of anguish carried on the wind. Some claim to have seen her standing atop the bridge, staring down into the waters below, as if searching for her lost love.

One such account comes from a local fisherman named Mehmet, who claims to have encountered the Weeping Woman on a warm summer evening in the late 1990s. As he cast his nets into the river, he suddenly heard the sound of a woman sobbing. Turning towards the bridge, he saw a figure clad in white, her long hair billowing in the breeze.

As Mehmet looked on, he felt a deep sense of sadness and could not help but be moved by the woman's sorrowful cries. As he approached her, the figure seemed to dissolve into the moonlight, leaving behind only the faint sound of weeping on the wind. Mehmet had no doubt that he had witnessed the spirit of the Weeping Woman, her pain and longing still echoing through the ages.

Another encounter comes from a group of tourists who visited the Malabadi Bridge in the early 2000s. While exploring the area, they began to hear the distant sound of a woman crying. Curious, they followed the sound, which led them to the foot of the bridge. There, they saw a woman dressed in white, her face hidden by a veil of tears. As they approached, the woman suddenly vanished, leaving the group in a state of shock and disbelief. They later learned of the legend of the Weeping Woman and were convinced that they had come face to face with her restless spirit.

Over the centuries, countless visitors to the Malabadi Bridge have reported similar experiences, all bearing witness to the tragic tale of Leyla and her eternal sorrow. Locals have come to accept the presence of the Weeping Woman, seeing her as a symbol of the bridge's storied past and the human emotions that are forever intertwined with its stones.

The Malabadi Bridge, with its rich history and architectural splendour, has stood the test of time, a silent witness to the joys and sorrows of the people who have crossed it. The story of the Weeping Woman serves as a haunting reminder of the depths of love and the lengths to which some will go to possess it. It is a tale of tragedy, betrayal, and the enduring power of the human spirit, a story that will forever be etched in the hearts and minds of those who dare to cross the haunted bridge of Malabadi.

The Phantom Car of Tuen Mun Road - Hong Kong

Hong Kong, a bustling metropolis known for its glittering skyline and vibrant culture, is no stranger to urban legends and eerie tales. Among these stories is the chilling account of the Phantom Car of Tuen Mun Road, a ghostly vehicle said to haunt the bridge along this busy expressway. The Tuen Mun Road, which connects the New Territories with Kowloon, is notorious for its high number of traffic accidents and fatalities, making it one of the most dangerous roadways in Hong Kong. This grim reputation has given rise to tales of supernatural occurrences and mysterious forces at work, with the Phantom Car being one of the most intriguing and terrifying.

The Tuen Mun Road Bridge was completed in 1978 as part of a larger infrastructure project aimed at improving transportation and connectivity within Hong Kong. The bridge, an impressive structure spanning the Tuen Mun River, was designed to withstand the demands of the rapidly growing population and the heavy traffic that plied the route. However, since its completion, the bridge has been the site of numerous accidents, some of which have been attributed to the enigmatic Phantom Car.

According to legend, the Phantom Car appears without warning, often late at night or during periods of poor visibility. Witnesses describe the vehicle as an old-fashioned, black sedan, with no discernible licence plate or identifying marks. The car is said to be driven by an unseen force, its windows shrouded in darkness, preventing any glimpse of its occupants, if indeed there are any. It is believed that the Phantom Car's appearance is an omen of impending doom, heralding accidents and misfortune for those who encounter it.

One harrowing account of the Phantom Car comes from a taxi driver named Mr. Wong, who experienced a chilling encounter on the Tuen Mun Road Bridge in the early 2000s. On a foggy night, as he drove along the bridge, Wong noticed a black sedan suddenly appear in his rearview mirror, seemingly out of nowhere. The car began tailgating him, its headlights casting an eerie glow through the thick fog. Fearing for his safety, Wong sped up, attempting to distance himself from the menacing vehicle. However, the Phantom Car kept pace, staying uncomfortably close to his bumper.

Suddenly, the black sedan swerved into the adjacent lane and accelerated, drawing level with Wong's taxi. As he glanced nervously at the car, he realised that there was no driver behind the wheel, only an impenetrable darkness where the driver should have been. Panicked, Wong slammed on the brakes, allowing the Phantom Car to speed past him and disappear into the fog. Shaken by the experience, Wong firmly believes that he encountered the ghostly vehicle that has haunted Tuen Mun Road for decades.

Another unsettling account comes from a group of friends returning home after a late-night gathering. As they crossed the Tuen Mun Road Bridge, they noticed a black sedan following closely behind them. The car's headlights were off, making it difficult to discern any details about the vehicle or its driver. Unnerved by the car's strange behaviour, the driver of the group's car decided to speed up, hoping to leave the mysterious vehicle behind.

To their horror, the black sedan began to accelerate as well, staying just a few metres behind them. As they reached the end of the bridge, the Phantom Car suddenly veered off the road and vanished, leaving the terrified friends in a state of shock and disbelief. They later learned of the legend surrounding the Tuen Mun Road Bridge and are convinced that they had a brush with the infamous Phantom Car.

As more and more stories of the Phantom Car began to surface, some residents and investigators started to search for a possible explanation for these supernatural encounters. Some believe that the Phantom Car could be a residual haunting, the spirit of a vehicle involved in a tragic accident that left a powerful imprint on the Tuen Mun Road Bridge. Others suggest that it might be a malevolent entity, deliberately causing chaos and misfortune for those who cross its path.

In an attempt to understand the origins of the Phantom Car, local researchers delved into the history of the Tuen Mun Road and the bridge itself. They discovered that during the construction of the road, several accidents had occurred, resulting in the loss of life for some of the workers. Could it be that the spirits of those who perished during the construction now haunt the bridge, manifesting themselves as the ominous Phantom Car?

Regardless of the true nature of the Phantom Car, the tales of its ghostly presence on the Tuen Mun Road Bridge continue to be a source of fascination and fear for those who travel along the busy expressway. The high number of accidents and fatalities only serve to reinforce the legend, lending an air of mystery and danger to the otherwise mundane structure.

As we delve deeper into the haunted bridges of the world, it becomes clear that each of these structures holds a unique and chilling tale, rooted in the history and culture of the places they connect. The Phantom Car of Tuen Mun Road is just one of many such stories, a ghostly reminder of the tragic events that have unfolded along the bridge and a testament to the unexplained phenomena that continue to defy explanation. For those who dare to venture along the Tuen Mun Road Bridge at night, the possibility of encountering the Phantom Car remains a haunting and terrifying prospect, one that will linger in their minds long after they have left the bridge behind.

The Haunted Humber Bridge - Hull, England

The Humber Bridge, a remarkable feat of engineering that spans the Humber Estuary, connecting the East Riding of Yorkshire with North Lincolnshire in England, has long been a source of fascination and wonder for locals and visitors alike. When it opened in 1981, it was the longest single-span suspension bridge in the world, a title it held until 1998. However, behind the impressive statistics and the stunning views that stretch across the estuary, there lies a darker, more mysterious side to this iconic structure.

Many who have crossed the Humber Bridge claim to have encountered strange, unexplained phenomena, from eerie sensations and disembodied voices to full-blown apparitions. Some even believe that the bridge is haunted by the spirits of those who have met a tragic end there. In this chapter, we will delve into the haunted history of the Humber Bridge, uncovering the chilling tales that have come to define this seemingly ordinary structure.

To understand the paranormal activity that has been reported on the Humber Bridge, it is essential to explore its history. The idea of a bridge spanning the Humber Estuary was first proposed in the early 20th century, but it was not until the 1960s that the project began in earnest. The construction of the bridge was a monumental undertaking, involving thousands of workers and years of planning and effort. Tragically, during the construction process, several workers lost their lives, and many believe that their spirits now haunt the bridge.

One of the most frequently reported ghostly encounters on the Humber Bridge involves a mysterious figure dressed in old-fashioned work clothes, who has been spotted wandering along the bridge's pedestrian walkway. According to eyewitness accounts, this spectral figure appears to be searching for something or someone, and those who have encountered him describe an overwhelming feeling of sadness and despair. Some speculate that this spirit may be one of the workers who perished during the bridge's construction, forever trapped in the place of his untimely death.

Another eerie tale associated with the Humber Bridge concerns the ghost of a woman dressed in white who has been seen walking along the bridge late at night. Those who have encountered this apparition describe her as having a serene, almost ethereal quality, and many believe that she is the spirit of a woman who took her own life by jumping from the bridge. There have been several reports of motorists stopping their cars, believing that they have seen a woman about to jump, only for her to vanish before their eyes.

In addition to the ghosts of the construction worker and the woman in white, there have been numerous reports of strange, unexplained phenomena occurring on the Humber Bridge. Some visitors have described hearing eerie whispers and disembodied footsteps, while others have experienced sudden drops in temperature or an inexplicable feeling of unease. These occurrences have led many to speculate that there may be more spirits haunting the bridge than just those who have met a tragic end there.

The haunted history of the Humber Bridge has been well documented, with countless eyewitness accounts and paranormal investigations attempting to uncover the truth behind the strange occurrences that have come to define this remarkable structure. In one notable investigation, a group of paranormal enthusiasts spent the night on the bridge, armed with recording equipment and infrared cameras in the hopes of capturing evidence of the supernatural activity that has been reported there.

During their investigation, the group reported several unexplained occurrences, including strange noises, sudden drops in temperature, and the overwhelming feeling of being watched. At one point, their recording equipment picked up a series of chilling, disembodied whispers that seemed to echo through the night air. Although the group was unable to definitively prove the existence of ghosts on the Humber Bridge, their experiences only served to fuel the speculation and intrigue surrounding this haunted structure.

As we explore the haunted bridges of the world, it is important to remember that each structure has its own unique history and tales that contribute to its eerie reputation. The Humber Bridge is no exception, and the chilling encounters experienced by those who have dared to cross it at night continue to captivate the imagination of believers and sceptics alike.

One particularly chilling account comes from a local man named

John, who was driving across the bridge late one evening. As he made his way along the empty stretch of road, he suddenly spotted a figure standing at the edge of the bridge. Concerned that the person was in distress, John pulled over and approached the figure, only to find that it was the ghostly woman in white that others had reported seeing.

As he watched in disbelief, the apparition seemed to float off the edge of the bridge and vanish into the darkness below. John later reported that the encounter left him feeling shaken and disoriented, and he has since been unable to shake the image of the woman in white from his mind.

Another eyewitness account comes from a woman named Jenny, who was walking along the pedestrian walkway of the Humber Bridge with her dog late one evening. As they made their way across the bridge, Jenny's dog suddenly began to growl and bark, seemingly at nothing in particular. Just then, Jenny felt a sudden drop in temperature and noticed a dark, shadowy figure standing several feet away from her.

Frightened, she quickly picked up her dog and began to make her way back towards the safety of the shore, all the while feeling as though she was being watched by the mysterious figure. When she finally reached her car, she glanced back at the bridge, only to see the shadowy figure had vanished without a trace.

These accounts, along with countless others, serve to paint a haunting portrait of the Humber Bridge and the mysterious spirits that are said to lurk within its shadows. From the tragic tales of those who have lost their lives there to the strange, unexplained phenomena experienced by those who have dared to cross it, the Humber Bridge is a fascinating example of the supernatural connections that can be found in even the most seemingly ordinary structures.

The Possessed Doll Bridge - Xochimilco, Mexico

In the heart of Xochimilco, Mexico, lies a place unlike any other, an island shrouded in mystery and terror. The Island of the Dolls, or Isla de las Muñecas, is home to countless eerie dolls hanging from the trees, their lifeless eyes watching over the island's haunted bridge. The story of this chilling location is steeped in tragedy, folklore, and supernatural encounters that defy explanation. In this chapter, we will venture into the dark history of the Possessed Doll Bridge, uncovering the chilling tales that have come to define this otherworldly place.

The origins of the Island of the Dolls can be traced back to the 1950s when a man named Don Julian Santana moved to the island to escape society and live in solitude. It wasn't long before he discovered the lifeless body of a young girl floating in the canals near his home. Haunted by the tragic death, Don Julian began to collect dolls in an attempt to appease her restless spirit.

He would hang the dolls from the trees around the island, their vacant eyes bearing witness to the strange events that would soon unfold.

As the years passed, Don Julian continued to collect dolls, many of which he found floating in the canals, discarded by their previous owners. The collection grew, and the island became a macabre spectacle, drawing the curious and the brave to witness the hundreds of dolls that hung from the trees. The Possessed Doll Bridge, the main access point to the island, soon became the focal point of the paranormal activity that seemed to permeate the area.

Many visitors to the island have reported feeling an overwhelming sense of dread as they approach the bridge, as if they are being watched by unseen forces. Some have even claimed to see the dolls move, their heads turning to follow visitors as they make their way across the bridge. Others have reported hearing whispers and disembodied laughter, the ghostly echoes of the children who once played with the dolls.

One chilling encounter comes from a man named Carlos, who visited the island with a group of friends, hoping to experience the supernatural phenomena that had become synonymous with the Possessed Doll Bridge. As they made their way across the bridge, Carlos noticed that one of the dolls seemed to be staring directly at him. He dismissed the feeling as a trick of the light, but as he continued to walk, he couldn't shake the feeling that the doll was watching him. Suddenly, he felt a cold hand on his shoulder and turned to find the doll had moved, its lifeless eyes staring into his soul. Carlos and his friends fled the island, vowing never to return.

The Possessed Doll Bridge is also said to be haunted by the spirit of Don Julian himself. In 2001, Don Julian was found dead in the same spot where he had discovered the young girl's body all those years ago. Locals believe that his spirit now lingers on the island, watching over the dolls and the bridge that has become synonymous with his legacy.

One such encounter with Don Julian's spirit comes from a woman named Maria, who visited the island with her husband in search of adventure. As they crossed the Possessed Doll Bridge, Maria felt a sudden chill in the air and turned to see the ghostly figure of an old man, believed to be Don Julian, standing at the edge of the bridge. The apparition beckoned to her before disappearing into the darkness, leaving Maria feeling both terrified and awestruck by the experience.

Over the years, the Possessed Doll Bridge has become the subject of numerous paranormal investigations, with teams of researchers attempting to unravel the mysteries that surround this eerie location. Some investigators have captured chilling photographs of the dolls, their eyes seeming to follow the camera as it moves. Others have recorded unexplained sounds, such as whispers, laughter, and footsteps, that seem to emanate from the dolls themselves. Despite the abundance of evidence and eyewitness accounts, sceptics remain unconvinced, attributing the strange occurrences to the power of suggestion and the eerie atmosphere of the island.

Nonetheless, the Possessed Doll Bridge continues to draw visitors from around the world, each hoping to catch a glimpse of the supernatural phenomena that have come to define this haunting place. Many have left with stories of their own, adding to the ever-growing legend of the Island of the Dolls and its chilling bridge.

One such story comes from a group of college students who ventured to the island on a dare. As they crossed the bridge, they couldn't help but feel unnerved by the countless dolls watching their every move. As they reached the centre of the bridge, they decided to take a group photo to commemorate their visit. When they later reviewed the photograph, they were horrified to see that several of the dolls appeared to have moved, their heads turned in unnatural angles, as if they were posing for the camera.

Another harrowing tale comes from a tourist named Emily, who visited the island with her family. As they walked across the Possessed Doll Bridge, Emily noticed one of the dolls, a small porcelain figure with long, tangled hair, seemed to be crying. Intrigued, she reached out to touch the doll, only to recoil in horror as the figure began to sob uncontrollably, tears streaming down its lifeless face. Emily and her family left the island shaken, unable to forget the chilling encounter.

As we explore the haunted bridges of the world, the Possessed Doll Bridge in Xochimilco, Mexico, stands out as one of the most enigmatic and terrifying. The stories that surround this haunting location, from the tragic tale of Don Julian and the young girl to the countless eerie dolls that watch over the bridge, serve as a chilling reminder of the supernatural forces that may lurk in the shadows of even the most seemingly ordinary structures.

In conclusion, the Possessed Doll Bridge is a testament to the enduring power of folklore and the unexplained phenomena that have captivated the human imagination for centuries. Whether you are a believer in the paranormal or a sceptic seeking thrilling tales, the chilling encounters and eerie atmosphere of the Island of the Dolls and its haunted bridge will undoubtedly leave a lasting impression on your mind, a haunting reminder of the mysteries that lie hidden within our world.

The Enigmatic Eshima Ohashi Bridge - Matsue, Japan

A striking and awe-inspiring structure, the Eshima Ohashi Bridge in Matsue, Japan, is a marvel of modern engineering. Stretching over a mile in length and rising to a staggering height, this impressive bridge connects the cities of Matsue and Sakaiminato and spans the breathtaking Lake Nakaumi. While many view this architectural feat as a symbol of progress and human ingenuity, others believe that the bridge holds a darker, more sinister secret. Local folklore and chilling eyewitness accounts suggest that the Eshima Ohashi Bridge is haunted, with mysterious spirits lurking in its shadowy corners, waiting to reveal themselves to unsuspecting passersby.

To understand the eerie tales that surround this magnificent bridge, one must delve into its history and the cultural context of the region. The Eshima Ohashi Bridge was completed in 2004, and its unique design, which features a steep incline on both sides, quickly earned it the nickname "Roller Coaster Bridge." This remarkable structure has become a popular tourist attraction, drawing visitors from all corners of the globe to marvel at its gravity-defying appearance.

The region surrounding the Eshima Ohashi Bridge has a rich and storied past, with many local legends and myths passed down through generations. One such tale is that of the Yurei, or the ghostly spirits that are believed to inhabit various locations throughout Japan. According to legend, these spirits are the souls of individuals who have suffered tragic or untimely deaths, and they are said to wander the world of the living, unable to find peace. It is these restless spirits that are believed to haunt the Eshima Ohashi Bridge, drawn to the towering structure by some unknown force.

Numerous eyewitness accounts have emerged in recent years, detailing encounters with these spectral beings on the bridge. One such story comes from a group of young travellers who had stopped to take photographs of the stunning view from the bridge's peak. As they captured the breathtaking panorama, they noticed a strange figure standing at the edge of the bridge. The figure appeared to be a woman, her long, flowing hair obscuring her face as she gazed out over the water. Intrigued, the group approached the woman, only to watch in horror as she vanished before their very eyes. The travellers were left shaken, unable to explain the chilling encounter they had just experienced.

Another tale comes from a local fisherman, who claims to have witnessed a ghostly procession of spirits marching across the Eshima Ohashi Bridge late one night. The fisherman was out on the water, his boat gently rocking in the calm lake when he spotted the eerie sight. He described the figures as translucent, their forms shimmering in the moonlight as they moved in unison across the bridge. He could hear the faint sound of their footsteps, echoing through the still night air. Unable to tear his eyes away from the spectral display, the fisherman watched as the spirits disappeared into the darkness, leaving him with a haunting memory he would never forget.

The stories of the haunted Eshima Ohashi Bridge have captured the attention of paranormal investigators and enthusiasts alike, with many attempting to unravel the mystery of the bridge's ghostly inhabitants. Some have theorised that the spirits are drawn to the bridge's unique design, as its steep incline and towering height create an otherworldly atmosphere that seems to defy the laws of nature. Others believe that the bridge's location, situated between two cities and spanning the vast Lake

Nakaumi, serves as a sort of spiritual crossroads, attracting lost souls from all corners of the region.

As the legend of the haunted Eshima Ohashi Bridge continues to grow, so too does the number of eyewitness accounts and chilling encounters. One such account comes from a truck driver who was making a late-night delivery across the bridge. As he navigated the steep incline, he noticed a figure standing near the edge of the bridge. Believing it to be a distressed person, he pulled his truck over and approached the figure to offer assistance. As he got closer, he realised that the person seemed to be hovering just above the ground, and their face was distorted in a ghastly expression. Terrified, the truck driver raced back to his vehicle and sped away, vowing never to cross the bridge again after dark.

Some locals have even claimed to experience strange, unexplained phenomena while on or near the Eshima Ohashi Bridge. One woman recalls driving across the bridge late one evening when her car suddenly stalled. As she attempted to restart the engine, she felt an icy cold breeze sweep through her vehicle, causing her to shiver uncontrollably. When she looked up, she saw the ghostly figure of a man standing just outside her car, his face twisted in anguish. The woman frantically restarted her car and sped away, too frightened to look back.

The Eshima Ohashi Bridge has also been the site of numerous accidents and unexplained incidents, which some believe are connected to the paranormal activity surrounding the bridge. In one such instance, a driver lost control of their vehicle and plunged into the lake below. The driver survived the harrowing ordeal but claimed to have seen ghostly figures floating above the water as they struggled to escape the sinking vehicle. The driver believes that these spirits may have played a part in the accident, causing them to lose control of their car and plummet into the depths below.

The haunted Eshima Ohashi Bridge continues to captivate and intrigue those who dare to venture across its awe-inspiring span. Its connection to local folklore and the numerous eyewitness accounts of ghostly encounters have cemented the bridge's reputation as a truly enigmatic and chilling location. As more and more people are drawn to the Eshima Ohashi Bridge to experience its haunting beauty and uncover its dark secrets, the bridge's paranormal legacy will undoubtedly continue to grow.

As we have traversed the world's spookiest structures and delved into the chilling secrets that lie within, we are left with a profound sense of wonder and unease. The haunted bridges we have explored serve as a stark reminder that the world is a mysterious and complex place, filled with secrets that defy explanation. As we go forth, we must embrace the unknown and keep an open mind, for the world is filled with hidden corners and uncharted territories that are just waiting to be discovered.

The Eshima Ohashi Bridge and its connection to the spectral world of Japanese folklore serve as a testament to the power of human imagination and our deep-rooted fascination with the unknown. As you cross this enigmatic bridge, you may find yourself pondering the delicate balance between the world of the living and the realm of the spirits, and the enduring mysteries that lie at the heart of our collective consciousness. Whether you are a believer in the paranormal or a sceptic seeking thrilling tales, the haunted Eshima Ohashi Bridge will surely leave a lasting impression on your psyche and may even inspire you to explore the countless other haunted bridges that dot the globe.

Afterword

As our spine-chilling journey across the world's haunted bridges comes to an end, we are left with a profound sense of wonder, unease, and perhaps even a touch of scepticism. The stories we have encountered throughout this book, ranging from ancient folklore to inexplicable encounters with the supernatural, have taken us on a voyage into the unknown, opening our eyes to the hidden and mysterious facets of the world. The haunted bridges we have explored have served as a reminder of the complexity and enigma that lies at the heart of our collective consciousness, and as we go forth, we must embrace the unknown and keep an open mind, for the world is filled with hidden corners and uncharted territories that are just waiting to be discovered.

These haunted bridges, spanning from Niagara Falls to Albuquerque and Matsue, Japan, have provided us with a rich tapestry of tales that are both captivating and terrifying. As we have delved into their histories and explored the eyewitness accounts of ghostly encounters, we have also come to understand the cultural significance and symbolism that these structures hold. Bridges, in their essence, symbolise the connections we make with others, the overcoming of obstacles, and the defiance of the natural world. They are the physical manifestations of our desire to conquer the unknown and to forge new paths in our lives. In this sense, haunted bridges serve as a stark reminder of the fragility of human existence and our never-ending quest for understanding and knowledge.

Throughout our exploration of the world's spookiest structures, we have encountered a wide range of supernatural phenomena, including tormented spirits, sinister beings, and mysterious occurrences that defy logical explanation. These chilling encounters have not only left us questioning our understanding of the world but have also provided us with valuable insights into the human psyche and our deep-rooted fascination with the unknown.

As we have traversed the globe and uncovered the chilling secrets that lie within these haunted bridges, we have also discovered a common thread that weaves its way through each of these tales. The stories we have encountered are, in many ways, a reflection of the fears, hopes, and desires of the people who have experienced them. They are a testament to the power of human imagination and our innate need to make sense of the world around us. In this sense, haunted bridges serve as a mirror through which we can glimpse the complexities of human nature and the universal yearning for connection and understanding.

As we ponder the tales we have encountered in this book, we must also acknowledge the role that scepticism and critical thinking play in our exploration of the unknown. While some may be quick to dismiss these stories as mere fabrications or the products of overactive imaginations, it is important to remember that the paranormal and the unexplained have long been a part of human history and culture. Throughout the ages, people have sought answers to life's mysteries, and the supernatural has often been a source of both fascination and fear.

It is our responsibility, as inquisitive and open-minded individuals, to approach these stories with a healthy dose of scepticism while also acknowledging the possibility that there may be more to these tales than meets the eye. By maintaining a balanced perspective and a willingness to explore the unknown, we can gain valuable insights into the human experience and the mysteries that continue to elude our understanding.

As we close the final chapter of "Haunted Bridges: Eerie

Encounters from The World's Spookiest Structures," we are left with a profound sense of curiosity and a desire to delve even deeper into the realm of the unknown. Whether we are believers in the paranormal or sceptics in search of thrilling tales, the haunted bridges we have explored have provided us with a rich and diverse array of stories that have both captivated and challenged our beliefs.

Our journey has only just begun, and as we continue to explore the hidden mysteries of the world, we may find ourselves drawn to other haunted locations and uncovering more chilling tales that defy explanation. We are left with a sense of wonder, as we ponder the countless mysteries that lie hidden within the shadows of our world. The stories we have encountered in this book are but a small fraction of the countless haunted places that exist across the globe, each with its own unique and terrifying tale to tell.

In this spirit of exploration and discovery, let us continue to seek out the unknown, embrace the mysteries that surround us, and maintain an open mind as we venture into the dark corners of our world. Whether we are investigating haunted forests, abandoned asylums, or other eerie locales, we can find solace in the fact that we are not alone in our curiosity and desire to understand the enigmatic.

While the bridges we have explored in this book have served as a testament to the power of human imagination, they have also provided us with valuable insights into the complex nature of fear and our innate desire to confront the unknown. As we forge new connections with others and continue to challenge the boundaries of our understanding, we can take comfort in the knowledge that our fascination with the paranormal and the unexplained is a shared experience that transcends cultures, time, and space.

As we move forward and leave the haunted bridges behind, let us embrace the unknown with open arms and an open heart, for it is through our exploration of the mysteries that surround us that we may find the answers we seek and gain a deeper understanding of ourselves and the world in which we live. So, as you close this book and venture forth into the great unknown, remember the haunted bridges and the chilling tales that have both captivated and challenged your beliefs. Carry with you the spirit of curiosity, scepticism, and wonder, and let it guide you on your journey through the shadows of our world, as you continue to seek out the unexplained and unravel the mysteries that lie hidden within.

Thank you for buying this book.

For more books by this author, just search "Lee Brickley" on Amazon.